MASTERING

HACKING

The Art of Information Gathering & Scanning

Harsh Bothra

Ethical Hacker & Independent Security Researcher

Technology Enthusiast | Author | Speaker | Trainer

KHANNA BOOK PUBLISHING CO. (P) LTD.

Publisher of Engineering and Computer Books

4C/4344, Ansari Road, Darya Ganj, New Delhi-110002

Phone : 011-23244447-48 **Mobile:** +91-9910909320

E-mail : contact@khannabooks.com

Website : www.khannabooks.com

Dear Readers,

To prevent the piracy, this book is secured with HIGH SECURITY HOLOGRAM on the front title cover. In case you don't find the hologram on the front cover title, please write us to at contact@khannabooks.com or whatsapp us at +91-99109 09320 and avail special gift voucher for yourself.

Specimen of Hologram on front Cover title:

Moreover, there is a SPECIAL DISCOUNT COUPON for you with EVERY HOLOGRAM.

How to avail this SPECIAL DISCOUNT:

Step 1: Scratch the hologram
Step 2: Under the scratch area, your "coupon code" is available
Step 3: Logon to www.khannabooks.com
Step 4: Use your "coupon code" in the shopping cart and get your copy at a special discount
Step 5: Enjoy your reading!

Price : ₹ 199.00

ISBN: 978-93-86173-84-3

Mastering Hacking
by Harsh Bothra

First Edition: 2019
Revised Edition: 2021
Reprint: 2023, **2025**

Published by:
Khanna Book Publishing Co. (P) Ltd.
Visit us at: **www.khannabooks.com**
Write us at: **contact@khannabooks.com**
CIN: U22110DL1998PTC095547

To view complete list of books, Please scan the QR Code:

Printed in Bharat.

MASTERING
HACKING
The Art of Information Gathering & Scanning

Special Thanks

Mr. Devansh Bordia

For his active contribution to this title & especially chapters: ***Networking & Enumeration.***

Please Note – You can find list of all the links mentioned in this book at: www.cybersquareinfo.com/masteringaigs

DISCLAIMER

This book is for education purpose only. The publisher and author do not motivate or support any unethical activity or use of the technology in an unethical way.

All the tools, technologies and methods demonstrated in the book are performed under a controlled and isolated environment. It is highly recommended to test only the public website(s) or take prior required permission(s) to test any websites.

The Author and Publisher are not responsible for any misuse/unethical use of the tools and methods demonstrated.

ACKNOWLEDGEMENTS

With the grace of Almighty God, I came up with another book after the launch of Hacking: Be A Hacker with Ethics.

I would like to especially thank my parents for always supporting me in all my decisions. I want to extend my thanks to my brother, sisters, brother – in – law and sister – in – law for always trusting in me & my works. To all the junior champs, my nephew and niece, lots of love to make my time refreshing with childishness.

I extend my hearty thanks to all my friends, teachers and all the persons who stood beside me, no matter what.

A Special thanks to **Mr Mukul Seth** & **Khanna Publishing House** in always trusting my works and providing me with support like a brother.

PREFACE

We are exponentially adapting the digital era and moving our business, daily lifestyle and activities towards the world of internet. Digital Assets are continuously increasing, and thus, there is a massive requirement of securing digital assets and protecting information.

Especially the young generation is getting much involved in social media and are quickly get into online frauds and scams, which sometimes leads to severe crimes and suicide. According to a survey, a considerable amount of youth is a victim of cyber bullying and torture. Some of the most common heard cases are, image morphing, sharing private video, spreading adult content and blackmailing over such things. There are many companions started about protecting sensitive data to aware the general public.

Digital Assets, Privacy, Information & Data, is also a concern of national security. The war is of data these days a and we are hearing a massive data breaches, especially from year 2018. The most famous companies like Facebook, UIDAI got victim of a massive data breach. Between all this, along with the general awareness of the security practices and protection strategies in the general public, we require to prepare them with better practices to learn cyber security & defence mechanism which would help them to protect against thefts, frauds and aware others in turn.

Cyber Security is the art of Digital Self Defence, the more you practise, the safer you become.

This book aims towards providing the best practices and methodology in the simplified approached, which would help both the technical and non-technical readers to learn and apply effectively. All the methods used are for the defence purpose and didn't intend to spread unethical activities.

Through this book, you would be able to learn about the modern Penetration Testing Framework, latest tools and techniques, discovering vulnerabilities, patching vulnerabilities, responsible disclosures and protecting assets over the network. This book tells about the uses and real-life applications of various techniques in depth and this acts as a handbook for your concrete step in information security.

CONTENTS

CONTENTS

ABOUT THE AUTHOR

Harsh Bothra is a Computer Science Engineer, Information Security Researcher & Ethical Hacker. He authored a book titled **Hacking: Be A Hacker with Ethics** recommended by MHRD, AICTE & NITTTR. Harsh is Founder & CEO of Cyber Square Info Solutions, Present Chapter leader of OWASP-Bikaner and former OWASP – Jaipur Chapter Lead for more than two years. He has been actively training students across various reputed institutions. Alongside, Harsh also works in developing software & web applications. Harsh has a significant interest in exploring various technical domains and spreading his knowledge through online & offline mediums.

PART-1

BUILDING THE BASE

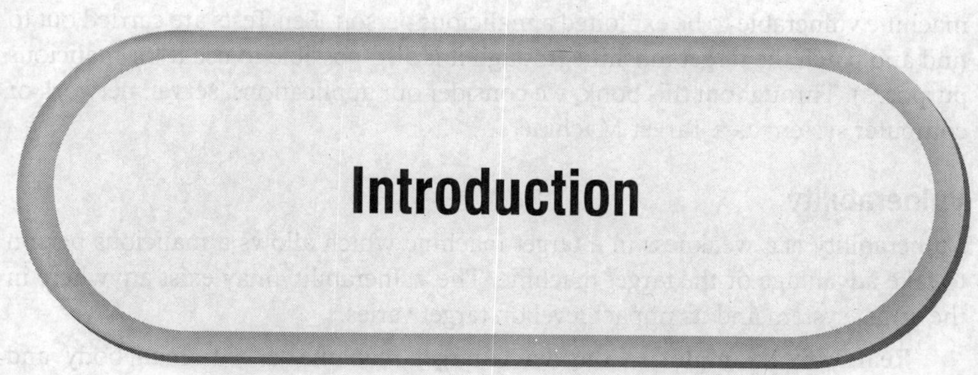

Introduction

Module Outlines

1. Overview of what you are going to learn throughout this book
2. Hacking & Penetration Testing in Broader Picture
3. The necessity of Information Intelligence

This book is emphasises on Information Intelligence. Since in the modern digital era, everything is dependent upon data & information is a useful piece of data. Information Intelligence is nothing but performing various activities/processes to gather Intel (Even more useful piece of information from existing Information), which can be used for the various purposes including Pattern Detection, Market Segment Analysis and Tracking Patterns in Crime & Frauds even in E-Commerce and Digital Mediums like Wallets, Websites & other E-Commerce & M-Commerce Applications.

Example – From a massive amount of data, after applying particular optimisation and other techniques, you have rendered a wide array of useful information. Assume, it is a dataset of People's Information. If you want to search for a specific person, then again You have to apply some processing to get more accurate results. Here, you are collecting **Intel about a Person from Available Dataset.**

You might wonder why you need such things to determine information about a person or related data. You can do it by conventional methods like crawling your contacts to get information about that person or asking your friends, but again, unintentionally, the process you are doing is Information Intelligence, think for a While and let's get started with learning.

Penetration Testing in a Bigger Picture

Penetration Testing often pronounced as pentesting or Pen Test is an art, science & technology of checking application, software, server, network or any target computer system against some vulnerability and exploiting the target by taking advantage of the discovered vulnerability. It mainly aims towards finding the loopholes which makes a computer system, application, network or any target machine vulnerable to be exploited a malicious person. Pen Tests are carried out to find and patch the target machine (though it is also possible to use it for malicious purposes). Throughout this book, we consider our applications, server, network or computer system as a Target Machine.

Vulnerability

Vulnerability is a weakness in a target machine which allows a malicious person to take advantage of the target machine. The vulnerability may exist anywhere in the target system and its impact level on target varies.

Real Life Example – Consider a target machine as a human body and immune system as a firewall. The body got a cut by the blade, and after few hours it developed an infection which turned out to be dangerous, that cut by blade acted as a vulnerability which allowed a virus to spread by fooling the immune system. Same happens in the digital world, the malicious code is injected into the weak points, which lead to compromising the target machine by fooling its firewall or security protocols.

Vulnerabilities varies according to the type of target system, for say, in a Web Application the significant vulnerabilities might look like HTTP Parameter Pollution, Local File Inclusion, Cross Site Scripting, Remote Code Execution wherein case of Network they might range from Denial of Service Attack, Brute Force Attacks, Missing Authentication and Authorization to OS Command Injections. There are many common vulnerabilities as well, which are found in almost all types of applications but in general, the high impact vulnerabilities varies according to the target. Hence, we require to deal with each vulnerability in a different manner, where some are easy to prevent while others take a lot of time and effort to manage.

There are several reasons which lead to developing vulnerabilities in a target system, some are –

1. Poor Code & Architecture Design
2. Improper Code Sanitization
3. Insecure Request & Response Handling
4. Lack of Tight Policies for User Authentication
5. Complex Applications
6. Access of the Network to Public
7. Outdated Technology and Plugins
8. Using default user credentials
9. Human Errors & Physical Damage, etc.

Hacking – Revealing the Myths

One of the biggest myths associated with Hacking and Hackers in our modern society is **Hacking/Hacker = Crime/Criminal.** Well, that's only a partial truth, a single side of a coin and it's not appropriate to judge a career or pathway.

Hacking is more of **an art, a tool, a process and method** of playing around digitally connected services whether web applications, mobile applications, hardware or iot enabled devices, anything digital. It involves Penetration Testing of a service, exploitation, maintaining access, performing the intended activity in the compromised service and getting out of the compromised service without leaving a single trace.

It can be done with good intents as well as bad, it is dependent upon the person sitting behind the screen and things cooking in his mind. There are many people who are using their skills for useful purpose, for securing the services by hacking and reporting to their developer/manufacturer, **The Ethical Hackers** and on the other hand, there are the people who are purposely hacking into services for their profit (might be financial or exploiting someone for personal reasons), **The Unethical Hackers.**

There is a vast society of Ethical Hackers and they are the backbone of your secure surfing over the internet, without the Ethical Hackers & Security Researchers, it's hard for the developers to secure their applications or services from the unwanted sources and data breaches which may impact both developers and its users. It was seen with many recent data breaches last year, here are some of the measures attached.

Most significant Data Breaches of 2018

1. **UIDAI (Aadhar Data Breach): 1.1Bn** user records compromised and leaked. Biggest Data Breach in history.
2. **Under Armour: 150Mn** user records breached.
3. **Facebook:** at least **87Mn** user records breached.
4. **Pump Up:** 6Mn user records breached.
5. **Saks, Lord & Taylor:** 5Mn user records breached including Credit & Debit Card details.

   (Data & Figure Source(s) – Internet)

The Necessity of Information Intelligence

As we have discussed in the previous section, what comprises of Information Intelligence or Intel Gathering. The point here is "Why we require Information Intelligence Practices", there are many options available to figure out the information required, the ultimate solution "Google Search" or "Phone – A – Friend". If we observe and think for a while, how Google search is working! What makes Google or any other search engine provide you with almost everything search result you ask. Yes, you thought it correct, **Information Intelligence.**

Every business or profession, whether online or offline, irrespective of anything, is dependent on Data & Information somehow. Data has become an essential part of the 21st century and thus giving rise to paths like Data Mining, Big Data, Data Science, Data Warehousing, Information Intelligence to name a few.

Information Intelligence plays Most significant role in almost every domain, specially in Information & Cyber Security and Forensics. Some of the major applications of Information Intelligence are:

1. It provides necessary information about the target system, which helps us to reduce and focus the scope of carrying out a test on Target.
2. It gives a basis for the Attack, *i.e.* It might help you to discover which service is running on target and you can use a vulnerable service to attack quickly.
3. Helps in Cyber Forensics and Cyber Crime & Fraud Investigation by gathering Intel about the suspects/victim or other information related to the investigation.
4. It helps Hackers to get information about the target organisation.
5. It can help Hacker to determine the Security Infrastructure of the Target.
6. Gives almost every information required to prepare for the attack/ perform test on the target system.

Throughout the process of Penetration Testing or Hacking, we rely upon the Information about the target system. Hence, it is essentially and efficient to gather as much as possible intel about the target system before setting up any exploitation or further process. This intel can be used to perform social engineering attacks as well, which sometimes is more successful and requires just human interaction. Throughout this book, we will learn various tools, techniques, methods and skills required for being expert in Information Extracting and at the end, we will look at how we can utilise the gathered information to hack into target system with ease.

It gives us a complete and broader picture of our target as well as a perfect scope and focus area for performing the pentest/hack.

Module Outlines

1. Introduction to Git
2. The various States of Git
3. Installing Git
4. Creating Git Repository & Other Commands
5. GitHub & GitHub Students Developer Pack

Git is one of the important tools for anyone who is into development, cyber security, data science, machine learning, engineering or any other activity requires open source interaction, collaboration and other stuff. In the beginning, it might sound something complex, but as you proceed through different sections, you get an exact picture about using and working with Git.

On the same hand, GitHub (recently owned by Microsoft) is built around Git as the base technology. We will first explore Git and its concept and moving forward with GitHub and at last if you are a student, GitHub Student Developer Pack. (something you must look at and avail.)

Git – Distributed Version Control System

Git is an open source system software, originally written by Linus Torvalds (creator of Linux) and is widely used and loved, especially by the developer's community. The idea behind Git was to promote open source, easy workflow and collaboration management, coordinating workflow between developers or organisation as a whole and tracking the changes made since initial development. Let's have a bigger picture about Git – the Distributed version control system

1. Free & Open Source
2. Distributed Version Control System
3. Track Development Changes
4. Efficiently manages workflow between Developers.
5. Easy Collaboration

6. Handles small to large project optimally and efficiently.
7. Multiple Workflows, Cheap Local Branching and convenient Staging areas.

Some of the well-known Organizations using Git –

1. Google
2. Facebook
3. Microsoft
4. Android
5. Netflix
6. LinkedIn
7. Linux
8. Twitter
9. KDE, and a long list to mention.

(source - https://git-scm.com/)

The Three States

The Three States is an important concept to remember about git. For the data or information used along with git, it contains mainly **Three States** for the git, *i.e.* –

1. Committed
2. Modified
3. Staged

Committed – It represents that after performing a particular task, the work has been updated and successfully stored in the local database (local filesystem). It just acts like saving a document.

Modified – When you are working on the data, and after performing a particular task, there is a modification in the data, and you haven't committed changes yet, this is a modified state.

Staged – It is a little non-conventional to understand, according to git, it means that you have marked a modified file in its current version to go into your next commit snapshot. In simple words, you add the file with modification(s) for commit in this state.

The simple workflow of git is, you **create a space in your local environment (working tree) and start playing around.** After the certain changes or further development, **the modified files in working tree are sent for the staging state and finally commit after the review and a latest snapshot of the changes is made permanent to the Git Directory** you are working on.

Installing Git

For installing git, we need to either clone or download the source file/ executables, and the installation process varies depending upon the various operating system(s). In this book, we will refer to the Installation process for Windows & Linux based systems. An additional link is provided for the MacOS and Source code installations.

Installing on Windows

1. Download Git for Windows (https://git-scm.com/download/win)
2. Open the Installer and follow the steps –
3. Click on Next > Next (select components window) > choose editor and click Next (if you are confused, keep default) > select path environment (Git from command line and also from 3rd party software) and click Next > Use the OpenSSL Library, hit Next > Next > Next > Install > Finish

Installing on Linux

- For Debian based distribution such as Kali or Ubuntu
  - **sudo apt install git-all**
- For Fedora or any other RPM based distributions such as RHEL or CentOS
  - **sudo dnf install git-all**
- For macOS & Source code installation –

  (https://git-scm.com/book/en/v2/Getting-Started-Installing-Git)

Creating Git Repository

A git repository is a location where you are going to store your files and code while working. It can be considered as a working directory.

The repository can be classified into two categories:

1. Local Repository – The repository in your local system environment.
2. Remote Repository – The repository placed somewhere on the internet or a server maybe far away from you which you can access remotely (over the network).

Similar to this there are two ways to create a git repository:

1. Create your local repository
2. Cloning a remote repository

Creating local repository:

- Ensure git is installed & configured.
- Open git terminal & perform following –
  1. cd <project location or place to store project>

     ex. cd /Desktop/MyRepo

2. **git init**

   this will initialize git and creates a new subdirectory **.git** which contains all the required repository files.

Cloning a remote repository:

- Ensure git is installed & configured.
- Open terminal & perform following –
  1. git clone <remote repo url>

     ex. git clone https://www.github.com/harsh_bothra/myRepo

     Throughout this book, while working on various open source tools and scripts, we will require to clone remote github repositories to use those tools. Though there is a way from where you can download the repository directly but working with the terminal is much faster and is one of the best practices. This book tries to provide you with best practices and help you understand core concepts in depth.

Some other useful git commands:

1. **git add <directory> -** after you perform changes in the project and ready to commit the changes, first you need to **stage**. This command is used for the same purpose. It stages all the changes in the project directory for next commit.
2. **git commit – m <message> -** It is used to commit the staged snapshot and -m flag is used to provide a message to notify other people what changes have been committed.
3. **git status** – shows the status of the current working repository with information like staged, unstaged and untracked files.
4. **git log** – displays the log files (history)
5. **git branch** – lists all the branches in your working repository.

GitHub

GitHub is one of the popular, widely used and largest host for the git repositories. Millions of developers are actively using github for their project collaboration, and many big organizations are also utilizing github for their most open source projects. According to GitHub website, it provides features like Code Review, Project Management, Integrations, Team Management, Social Coding, Documentation & Code Hosting. For more information - (www.github.com)

We encourage you to navigate to www.github.com and create an account, it is as simple as creating any other social media account and explore various features provided by the GitHub. You can create free public repositories and collaborate & contribute to other existing repositories if you are interested in. Since development and contribution are not out major thing to deal with, we will stick to our Information Intelligence.

GitHub Student Developer Pack

(https://education.github.com/pack)

GitHub Student Developer Pack is for the students who are enrolled into a valid full-time course in any university or school for their studies. Visit the link mentioned below section heading and get your pack by submitting basic details.

It will require you to fill out a basic form asking a few questions like how you will use this pack and so. Don't forget to use **academic email id & upload your valid ID Card. (both issued by your current academic institution)**

It has a wide variety of tools and other learning resources which are premium, but you will get all of them for free, and it's cool to explore all the resources.

There are many advanced concepts of git and are beyond the scope of this book. We intend to provide you with all the necessary details required for easy navigation and learning through this book.

If you are interested in learning git in – depth, refer –

https://git-scm.com/book/en/v2

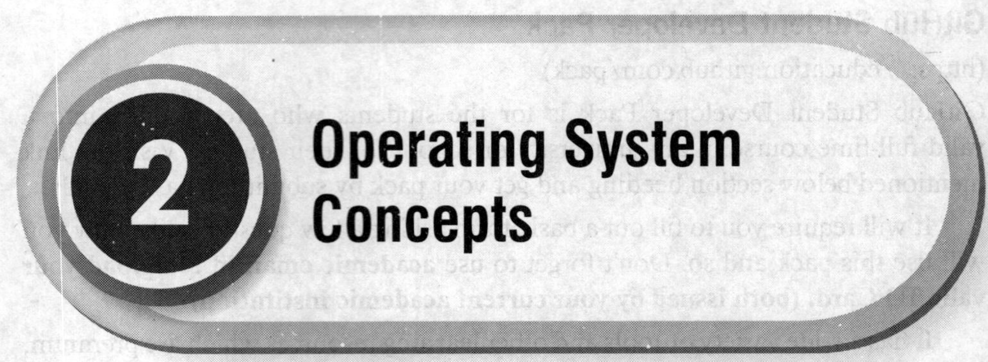

2 Operating System Concepts

Module Outlines

1. Introduction to Operating System
2. Operating System Modes
3. Fundamental Tasks of Operating System
4. Important terms in Operating System

Operating System is a very basic and an important concept to learn and practice. Daily, we interact with some operating system, like humans have their soul similarly, the operating system is driving force, the soul of the technology.

Whether you use Android Smartphone or an Apple iPhone, A Personal Computer (Windows Computers) or Linux/Mac based Computers, we interact with an interface which is user friendly and guide us with what to do. Similarly, there is a system which also guides the hardware and other components in our computing system. The interface or typically a piece of software which acts as a guide, regulator and operator for both users and computer hardware & internal logical processes is known as **Operating System.**

There are a wide variety of operating systems, most common and daily used operating systems are **Windows, Linux, MacOS, etc.** Android is a smartphone OS which is also based on Linux kernel (It is a component with fully unlocked features used to develop an operating system or the component from which operating systems are derived). Apart from this, many enterprises use RedHat Operating systems which are also based on Linux kernel.

Technically, Operating System is a software that manages and controls a computing device's core functionality such as managing the process, allocating resources to various services, storage allocation and management, memory (RAM) management, defining and ensuring security measurements, Interfacing (connecting link) between hardware and software, etc. All the smart devices like Laptops, PCs, Smart TVs, Smart Phones, etc. have some operating system to operate and interact with the end user.

Operating systems generally have two operation modes:

1. **Kernel Mode** – Full & Unrestricted Access to the Resources.
2. **User Mode** – Restricted Access and rules are defined on resources allocation & access.

Many well-known authors and internet mention different numbers of key tasks of an operating system. Let's divide them into **FIVE FUNDAMENTAL TASKS OF OPERATING SYSTEM:**

1. **Process Management** – The role of process management is to optimally manage the process(s) or task before/after the execution of a service or an application. When we execute a service or an application, many sub-process(s) initiates, and they must be optimally managed and also required to avoid deadlock situations.
2. **Memory Management** – Whenever a process executes, it occupies the space in memory for execution, the user has limited memory resources, and for smooth computing experience, it is necessary to manage memory, for the same operating system schedule process(s) through various methods.
3. **Device Management** – When we connect a hardware device to our computer system, it requires to understand the use and how to interact with the device, on which logical port it is to be connected and what service is to offer. The Operating System manages all of this, and ensures that all the device(s) function properly.
4. **Storage Management** – Storage refers to the disk space and task in storage management is disk space allocation. User need to store files or data on the computer, and it consumes disk space, to maximize data storage, avoid corruption and fragmentation in data, it is required to manage storage, and the operating system does this job well.
5. **User Interface** – Operating System provided an interface for the user to interact with OS, and it is generally graphical so that user can interact with Ease. There are two types of interfaces –
   a. Graphical User Interface (GUI)
   b. Command Line Interface (CLI)

Important Terms in Operating System

1. **Deadlock** – Deadlock is a phase where the processes involved die/never compete because of starvation *i.e.* suppose there are two process A and B. A requires a resource X to complete its execution but, B is utilizing X and can't free until B's execution is completed. At the same time, B requires some resource Y which is currently allocated to A, but A can't free until its execution is completed. Now both the processes A & B are waiting for resources X & Y to complete their execution and here **Deadlock** situation occurs.

2. **Stack** – It is a data structure which temporarily holds the data such as methods, functions, local variables, etc.
3. **Heap** – It is a data structure which represents **Dynamic Memory Allocation.**
4. **Thread** – It is a lightweight process which is used for improving service/process performance through process parallelism. The concept of multi-threading allows execution of multiple threads simultaneously. There are generally **User Level & Kernel Level Threads.**
5. **Direct Memory Access (DMA)** – It is used to reduce overhead. It can simply refer when CPU grants any Input/output (I/O) module, an authority to read/write to memory without any involvement. DMA Controller is known as DMAC.
6. **Virtualization** – It is a great technology which allows us to create multiple virtual copies of environments (like Operating Systems) on a single physical device. We will explore virtual machine thoroughly in the next chapter.

3 Networking Concepts

Chapter Outline

- Introduction to Computer Networks
- OSI/TCP Model
- IP Address & MAC Fundamentals
- Routing & Switching
- Connection Oriented vs Connectionless Networks
- Ports & TCP Flags
- Network vs Administrative Shares
- Network Protocols

During Penetration Testing, it is important for the attacker to know necessary network protocols and services to exploit vulnerabilities in the system. Networking is crucial in Pentest as it determine the common services, ports, protocols, IP, domain information to reveal information about the network architecture and configuration during an audit. So, we know why it is important to know the basics of computer networks let's get started with some basic definitions and terminology required for us to know to analyse the network architecture and help us to understand system services running on victim machine.

Network & Terminologies

Network: A computer network is defined as the interconnection of two or more devices having a different physical address which are communicating with each other through a medium having a set of rules and regulations required for each other to communicate with each other and access resources remotely from internet. The devices which are connected to the network and sharing resources within the network are called hosts or nodes. In simple terms, the devices that are used for controlling and directing the communication over the network are Network Devices and medium through which they can share resources and establish a connection with each other is decided on based on of communication medium. Protocols define how devices with different hardware and software can communicate also determines how the communication link is to establish with each other.

a. **Topologies:** Topology defines the physical arrangement and the layout pattern using which devices are interconnected such as Bus, Star, Mesh, Ring, Daisy chain.

b. **Hostname**: A hostname is unique identifier which is to identify network name which a device is going to be connected or even SSID(Service-Set-Identifier). To check the **hostname,** you can type hostname in cmd it will reveal the network name for the computer.

c. **Domain Name System (DNS):** The DNS is an internet directory which contains information about all the host and the associated IP address of each domain or server on the internet. It based on hierarchy model and contains the information about root servers, nameservers and top-level domain.

d. **Network Interface Card**: Network Interface Card is hardware which that helps users connecting to the network. It has physical address burned into it, which is used to identify host on the network.

e. **Components in Network:**
   - Nodes
   - Network Media & NIC
   - Network Devices

Open System Interconnect Model

Before getting started with the ISO-OSI Model, we should know why there is a need such model and what is used for. In 1984, an organisation known as ISO released a conceptual model called OSI model because different vendors, companies used different standards, protocols, form factors for communication purposes in computer networks. To ensure, national and worldwide data communication, systems must be developed which are compatible to communicate with each other ISO has developed a standard.

The ISO-OSI model is a **7-layer architecture.** It defines seven layers or levels in a complete communication system. They are:

1. Application Layer
2. Presentation Layer
3. Session Layer
4. Transport Layer
5. Network Layer
6. Data Link Layer
7. Physical Layer

Layer	Function	Example
Application (7)	Services that are used with end user applications	SMTP
Presentation (6)	Formats the data so that it can be viewed by the user Encrypt and decrypt	JPG, GIF, HTTPS, SSL, TLS
Session (5)	Establishes/ends connections between two hosts	NetBIOS, PPTP
Transport (4)	Responsible for the transport protocol and error handling	TCP, UDP
Network (3)	Reads the IP address form the packet.	Routers, Layer 3 Switches
Data Link (2)	Reads the MAC address from the data packet	Switches
Physical (1)	Send data on to the physical wire.	Hubs, NICS, Cable

Source-Blackmore Ops(Google Images)

Since we are familiar with the use of conceptual model let us now dive deep into how the information is exchanged from source to receiver. In every layer of this OSI model, the information is carried in a format which can be interpreted, recognized, decoded by the destination. Every layer has a standard format to prepare the data that is to send to the receiver. However, there is common structure used by every layer and is mainly divided into 2 parts:

1. **Header:** The header has protocol specific structure; this ensures that receiving host can interpret the message and handle the overall communication. It contains information that is required by the host to deliver the data to a destination such as destination address, port, service type, IP version, flags etc.
2. **Payload:** The payload contains actual data or information that is to be sent from source to destination. The size of the payload is limited, and data is to be sent in the form of chunks or small units by segmenting the packet in a defined sequence. The maximum size of payload that can send is 65535 bytes (TCP Layer).

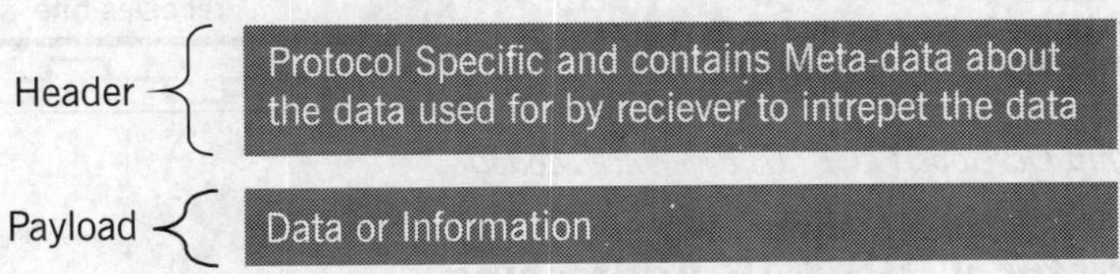

The most important point is to remember that every layer has its header. The packet is the basic unit of information transferred across a network, consisting, at a minimum, of a header with the sending and receiving hosts' addresses, and a body with the data to be transferred. As the packet travels through the TCP/IP protocol stack, the protocols at each layer either add or remove fields from the basic header. When a protocol on the sending host adds data to the packet header, the process is called **Data Encapsulation.**

TCP/IP Protocol Stack-Reference Model

TCP/IP that is Transmission Control Protocol and Internet Protocol were developed by Department of **Defence's Project Research Agency** (ARPA, later DARPA) as a part of a research project of network interconnection to connect remote machines. The simple concept was to develop a mechanism in which one computer running an application can talk to another machine running another application on a different network. The TCP/IP model was more robust and dynamic as compared to OSI and also included only 5 Layers which ensured that communication is easy and there is no congestion during the transmission of data from one network and to another network. The 5 Layers of the suite are:

1. Application Layer
2. Transport Layer
3. Internet Layer
4. Network Layer
5. Physical Layer

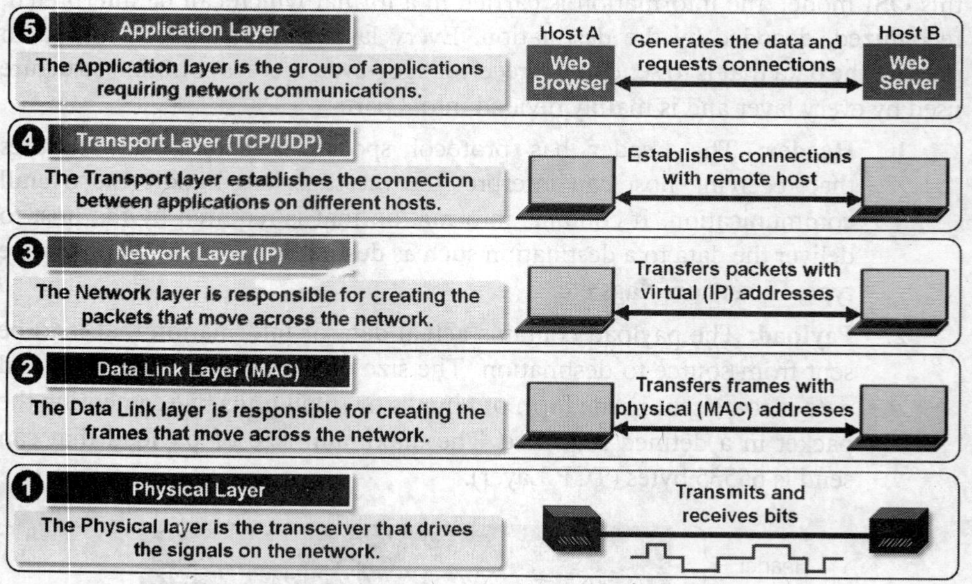

Source-Microchip Developer(TCP/IP Reference Model)

Internet Protocol (IP) & IP Addressing

Have you ever wondered how the devices are managed on the internet & how we keep track every device that is connected to a network? There should be a method to identify the host on the network and work with devices all the around the internet. Internet protocol is used at layer 3 of the OSI Model and is incharge of delivering the packets from source to destination network. It uses IP headers to recognize the recipient.

An **IP Address** is a unique address that is being assigned to every host or node on the network while being connected and is used to identify end devices on every network. The IP Address has majorly 2 versions:

1. IP-v4(32 bit)
2. IP-v6(128 bit)

1. IP-V4 Address

- IP-V4 address is a 32bit address which assigned to a node having 4 octets, each of 8 bits separated by a dot (.)

  e.g. 73.5.12.137

- The maximum value of an octet is 255, and the minimum value is 0.
- The device with default a IP address is 0.0.0.0
- NAT implementation is used.
- To find out your IP address in cmd type following command:

  e.g. Windows-Ipconfig

  Linux-ifconfig

- It follows binary number counting in the form of 0 and 1.
- The total no IP Address that can be used in this version is 4billion approx.

2. IPV-6 Address

- IP-V6 address has 128bit address which consists of 8 groups of 16bit hexadecimal values separated by colon (:)

  e.g. EF80: 0000: 0000: AB23: 781Q: 767C: 123D: 08A2

- The maximum value of the group can be up to
- NAT implementation is not used.
- Autoconfiguration capabilities and routing features.
- Stateless Auto Configuration (SLAAC) allows to creating internet routable address called Global Unicast Address (GUA) without DHCP Server.
- Link Local Address is used while communicating on the same network.

Types of IP Address

1. **Private Address:** There is a certain block of IP address which is reserved for private network or LAN. When a node or host is connected to the network, we assign only this address and access to the internet and resources is not accessible. It is used for the internal host IP addressing and mostly used in IPv4 address. The following are block of IP address used in private addressing are as follows:
   - 10.0.0.0-10.255.255.255
   - 172.16.0.0-172.16.255.255

- 192.168.0.0-192.168.255.255

2. **Public Address:** When a user wants to access a resource or internet, they must use an address which is internet routable assigned by Internet Service Provider (ISP) or globally routed address. **Hereby at this moment, we need the concept of Network Address Translation (NAT) which converts Private Address into Public Address so that we can access a resource or internet**. In simple terms, a private address is not allowed by ISP to access the internet and required to convert into a routable IP address.

IP Addressing Classes

- **Class A**: The IP address used in this block is from 0.0.0.0-127.255.255.255. The first 8 bits are used for network part and next 24 bits for the host. The default the mask is 255.0.0.0. There is a special block used in this class called loopback Address used for network diagnostics and troubleshooting. The address starts at 127.0.0.0-127.255.255.255. The default loop address for our device or node is 127.0.0.1.
- **Class B:** The IP address used in this block is from 128.0.0.0-191.255.255.255. The last 16 bits are used for host part and first 16 bits for network id. The default mask is 255.255.0.0. There address block used by when the available network blocks are completely used, or a situation arises where we cannot IP address to the device as the current pool of address is full or unavailable. The address used called Automatic Private IP Addressing (APIPA) used for this purpose and depicted by address block 169.254.0.0-169.254.255.255.
- **Class C:** This address block is commonly used as its most versatile, and logical address block used by the users because of host limitation capacity. The address starts block from 192.0.0.0-223.255.255.255. The 24 bits are reserved for network and last 8 bits are used for the host. The total no of logical address used in this address block is 254, and 2 address are generally broadcast address and default gateway(router). The default the subnet mask is 255.255.255.0.
- **Class D:** This block of address, is mainly used for the multicast purpose or experimental use. The network block used are 224.0.0.0-239.255.255.255.
- **Class E:** The addressing starts from 224.0.0.0-255.0.0.0.

Subnet Mask

The Subnet Mask or commonly known as netmask, is used for identifying the network and host part in the network. To completely identify a host on the on network, we need to know both the parts. A subnet is, logical division of network address block and subnetting is process or method of dividing network blocks into small chunks or sets of network blocks to perform network segmentation are increase the number of networks in an organisation. The main identifiers are only 2 parts

- Network ID
- Host ID

There are commonly 3 types of subnets address used which are commonly used /24, /16, /8. This / notation depicts the number of bits used in the network address part. Higher network bits used, more the number of logical networks created or higher subnets. This type of addressing used is called Classless IP addressing or CIDR (Classless Inter Domain Routing).

e.g. IP-192.168.1.1/24

Here the network ID-192.168.1.0 and 24 bits are used for determining the network address for this given IP address.

Media Access Control

To understand what really MAC is first we need to know how we connect to the network. To connect, we need physical network interface or NIC so that we can connect to network and can be assigned an IP address. This NIC is assigned a unique address which burned within itself or hardcoded within it to identify host or node on the network. This address is called the MAC address. It is 48-bit, hexadecimal address divided into six 8 bits blocks.

e.g. 90:48:E2:A7:B8:22

Key Differences between IP Address & MAC Address

1. IP Address is used to identify network address, and Mac Address helps to know the Physical Address of the device.
2. IP address works on Layer 3 where as Mac Layer works on Layer 2.
3. IP address is 32 bit, and MAC address is 48 bit.
4. IP Addressed can be assigned manually or dynamically.
5. MAC is used in hubs, switches, bridges and IP address used in Routers.

Network Routing

Routing is defined as a method of ensuring that packet sends from source will be received by the receiver as the packet is being transmitted from predefined path or route. It is used for selecting a path for traffic in a network across multiple networks. Routers are devices that are connected to different networks and are responsible for forwarding traffic or IP datagrams between multiple networks. The forwarding of packets is done on basis of certain policies called routing protocols. These protocols are used to determine the best path to reach the network.

The Functionality of Router

- Routers are Layer 3 devices that are used to forward traffic from one network to another.
- They are used to store the mapping of the network in the form of routing tables
- They ensure the best possible path for packet to be transmitted from one network to another.
- They are used to direct the traffic flow, manage congestion and drop packet with a broadcast address
- They analyse IP headers in order to transmit the packet between multiple networks.
- The routers are also called default gateway for a network because every packet has to travel to the router to go out of the network and communicate with different end devices.
- The main types of routing are static and dynamic. In static, the routing path is fixed or predetermined, whereas in dynamic routing, there are certain rules or policy that govern the network traffic flow and path that is used for communicating on different networks.
- Routers have a unique table or method to map the different network address. This table is called routing table, which contains information about different networks such as routes, IP, Metric, Gateway, Interface, Netmask. There is default entry in the table which consists address of unknown network called a default route with value of 0.0.0.0.

Structure of Routing Table

- Network ID
- Netmask
- Gateway
- Interface
- Metric

Network ID	Netmask	Gateway	Interface	Metric
192.168.1.0	255.255.255.0	192.168.1.1	1	55
10.0.1.0	255.255.255.0	10.0.1.1	2	313

Switching

Switches and Hubs are network device which operates at Layer 2 and deals with frames. The frame is protocol datagram unit for layer, and there is an addition of MAC address from the IP layer in TCP/IP stack. In switches, the traffic is handled by forwarding table that binds interfaces to MAC address. The table is Content Addressable Memory table which has finite size and structure present in ram of a switch. The values inside the CAM Table is constantly is updated or refreshed after certain interval of time depending on TTL values. The following is the structure of the CAM table:

CAM Table Structure

- MAC Address
- Time to Live
- Interfaces

MAC Address	TTL	Interfaces
00:11:22:33:44:45	30	1
10:E8:2A:B3:11:12	5	2

Operations performed in CAM Table

- If destination MAC address is present in CAM table, then its TTL value is updated and send to the receiver.
- If destination MAC address is not present in CAM table, then it automatically adds the MAC address with its interface by analysing frame headers.
- If destination MAC address is present in CAM table with different interface then switches the interfaces and add it to the table with the same TTL value.

Forwarding Policy

- The host sends the frames to destination MAC address via switch where it is interpreted.
- The switch performs a lookup in CAM table and checks for destination MAC.
- Then it forwards the frames to the destination address
- If there is no entry in CAM, then it will forward it to all the interfaces where the corresponding interface will interpret and read the frame.

Connection Oriented vs Connectionless Networks

To understand the concept of Connection Oriented networks, we must understand why there is a need of such type of networks. The TCP layer uses Connection Oriented networks because it ensures guarantee packet delivery feature and reliability. The communication between different systems is initiated until the connection is established, which is ensured by such type of network. This type of approach helps the sender to ensure that after the connection is established the payload is sent to the receiver and it sends an acknowledgement for knowing that packet is delivered. The major protocol used here is TCP which makes a connection and allow using sliding window protocol in order to control rate of flow of incoming traffic and manages the TCP window size to process the data being sent from the source. There are mainly 2 types of protocols used TCP, UDP used in the networks for delivery purposes. Now we have a basic idea of the connection-oriented network lets us understand the connectionless network, the UDP stands for User Datagram Protocol it is less reliable and does not guarantee packet delivery feature so that it is inconvenient to use UDP where data is a priority. UDP sends stream bits for sending data where there is no surety of packet being transmitted to the receiver also packet is loss during the transmission. This type of communication is used video streaming, VOIP.

Difference between TCP & UDP

TCP	UDP
Connection Oriented	Connection less
Reliable	Not Reliable
The TCP header size is 20 bytes	The UDP header size is 8 bytes
Sends Acknowledgment	Sends No Acknowledgment
Error Detection & Sliding Window protocol is used to control traffic and TCP window size.	Error detection is not present and no sliding window protocol used
Connection is slow and heavy	Connection is fast and light
Protocols used are FTP, HTTP, HTTPS, SMTP, Telnet	Protocols used are SNMP, DNS, DHCP, TFTP

Ports

Ports are a logical endpoint in communication between two different computer systems. The ports are used to identify network process or application and system services running to communicate with between application also transfer data back-forth between applications. The TCP layer uses a process-to-process delivery mechanism so that to listen and communicate on different network services, also share data between remote systems using this method. Ports are of mainly of 2 types physical and logical, but in this module, we are going deal logical ports and it's implementation how its used by the OS to ensure process-to-process or service-to-service delivery approach. There are 65536 ports in the computer systems. The Registration of these ports is maintained by authority Internet Assigned Numbers Authority (IANA). The good example would client-architecture where browser communicates both running different applications on different ports. The ports are classified into 3 parts:

- Well Known Ports (0-1023) – It is used for system services and reserved for process used by the operating system. Generally, network services or protocols uses this ports.
- Registered Ports (1024-49151) – They are used by different companies, vendors to run application or software services on this port.

- Ephemeral Ports (49152-65535) – They are used as source ports which are randomly assigned by the OS during communication and commonly runs a service which is not standard.
- A socket is a bi-directional communication channel which allows source and receiver to communicate with each other and also provides different application to transfer data through TCP/IP Stack. A socket can be used with a network or used for system service managed by OS to transfer data within applications and programs.
- The socket has 2 values <IP: PORT> which ensures this process-to-process communication between different applications.
  E.g. 192.168.43.1:443

Ports	Services
TCP 21	File Transfer Protocol
TCP 22	Secure Shell
TCP 23	Telnet
TCP 25	SMTP
TCP 53	DNS
TCP 80	HTTP
TCP 110	POP3
TCP 123	NTP
TCP 135	RPC
TCP 137	NetBIOS Naming Service (NBNS)
TCP 138	NetBIOS Datagram
TCP 139	NetBIOS TCP Session
TCP 143	IMAP
TCP 389	Light-weight Directory Access Protocol (LDAP)
TCP 443	HTTPS
TCP 445	SMB Over TCP
TCP 3289	Global Catalog Service
TCP 3389	Remote Desktop Protocol (RDP)

TCP FLAGS

The TCP flags are used to determine the connection state and also handles the payload by processing it between different application or services. The flags indicate how to process the data by OS and send it from one network to another.

It is used to allocate resources as OS needs to process this data. Processing data needs some resources in terms of memory, CPU time, process management etc. The flags can have only 2 values on or off. This value depicts whether the flag is set to be used or not. There are mainly 6 types of flags. TCP flags are also called control bits as control connection state information.

- SYN-It is used for the establishment of TCP conn and synchronisation as it initiates the connection between 2 different remote hosts.
- ACK-It is us used as acknowledgement for SYN flag and it informs the source that receiver is alive and listening on a port.
- URG- The urgent flag process data at topmost priority and stops all other process. The resources are allocated by OS to process the packet with URG set. The data is non-sequential and buffered data is cleared in the memory to process the URG flag packet.
- PSH- The PSH flag informs sending application in TCP that data should be sent immediately. The TCP header informs receiving host that data be processed immediately also sends data even when the buffer is not full.
- FIN-The fin flag terminates the connection and sends the last packet to receiver informing that conn must also be terminated no more data is to be sent during the session.
- RST-The flag reset the connection or break connection due to some internal network errors and TCP session is terminated. The RST flag informs about the port status whether port is open or closed. If port is closed then is RST flag is sent by the receiver.

Please Note

- There are 2 more flags associated with TCP flags CWR, ECE.
- Congestion Window Reduced (CWR), which indicates that due to network congestion, the queue of outstanding packets has been lowered.
- Explicit Congestion Notification Echo (ECE) informs that the network is going congestion

TCP Handshake

The TCP 3-way handshake is used to establish a connection between the remote host and also helps to know to connect a service or port on the remote system. The handshake determines whether server and machine are active or listening on a port for an incoming connection. If the handshake is done then the connection is established so the information or data can be sent on that port. The handshake uses mainly SYN, ACK flag and RST if the port is closed. We can divide handshake into three stages:

- The sender sends a packet with SYN flag enabled in order to establish a connection with the remote host on particular port with random sequence no X.

- The receiver replies to SYN flag with an acknowledgment, this depicts that the server is listening on incoming port and ready for connection. Here SYN|ACK Flag both are used in response with request being sent by the sender. The sequence no of ACK flag is set to Y=X+1, SYN=Z.
- The sender then finally sends the Acknowledgement or ACK flag only to ensure the connection is completed and data can be transmitted on that remote port. The client has connected to that port and depicting that port is open. The sequence no is changed to ACK=Z+1
- Finally, the data can be transmitted between remote host there is TCP session being created for transmission purpose.

Diagram of TCP-3 Way Handshake

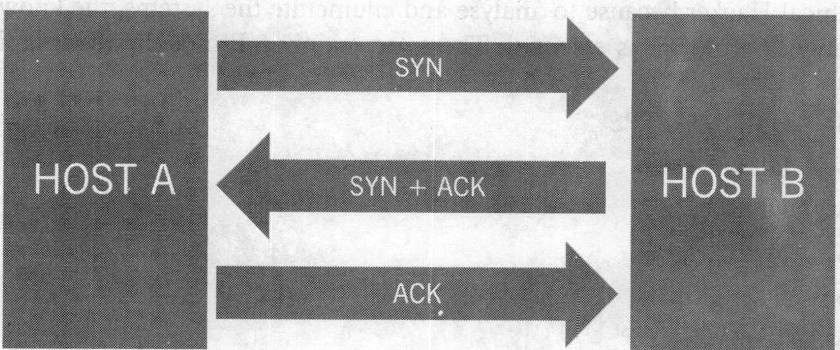

Network Shares

A share is defined as access to a resource such as a file, directory or any system services within a given network such that users in that network can read, access, connect, write changes within the computer hosting. Windows machine share file/directory on the network. This allows users to connect and view the share on the network. Sharing a resource means access to file which can be shared locally or remotely and also adding authentication on the share for security concerns so only intended users can access the share.

To access a network resource on the network and connect to it, users need a method or standard to access the share provided by Universal Naming Convention (UNC) Path. The syntax for UNC Path is: **\\SERVERNAME\Share Name\File Name**

Admin Shares

There are certain admin shares which can be accessed locally or by System Admin. This are restricted shares within the windows system and depicted by $ sign. Even if the shares are deleted, they are recreated by OS during the next bootup and are default system shares. The shares can be accessed by user typing command:**\\localhost\sharename**. There are 3 types of admin shares in the Windows system

- Local Drive or Disk Share(C$)-It allows the user to share default local disk or drive on the network. ex) C$, D$, E$.
- Admin Share (Admin$)-The share points or maps default windows installation directory
- Inter-Process Communication Share (IPC$)-This share allows IPC communication so that different programs can share resources and communicate with each other.

Network Protocols

The protocols are set of rules that are required by a network with different hardware and software configuration to communicate with each other to transmit resources and data from host to destination. There are different protocols we need to know as Ethical Hacker because to analyse and enumerate the systems, the knowledge of network protocols is essential. There are mainly 6 Protocols we are going to discuss in detail

- HTTP/HTTPS
- DHCP
- DNS
- NetBIOS
- FTP & SMB
- Telnet & RDP

Hypertext Transfer Protocol (HTTP)

HTTP is defined as Hypertext Transfer Protocol which is standard way of communicating and requesting for websites over the internet. It is the most common protocol used on the web and responsible for fetching and displaying the contents of the webpage by using request-response cycle. It is application layer protocol used and is not secure as the data is being transmitted in plain-text or clear text which can be easily eavesdropped by hacker to sniff the credential over the network.

Features of HTTP

1. HTTP is a stateless protocol it means every request is independent of itself because stateless protocol does not require the server to retain session information or status about each communications partner for the duration of multiple requests. HTTP is a stateless protocol, which means that connection between the browser and the server is lost after the response.
2. HTTP is a plain-text protocol which means the communication between the website and the server is not encrypted or data is sent across the network in clear text (without any transformation).

3. It works on request-response cycle that means if the client wants to access a particular resource on the remote server then must send a HTTP request which is standard used by clients to form a valid HTTP request according to RFC2616 and sends it to server in using URL (Uniform Resource Locator) and it is interpreted by sever and send the resource in the form of HTML and response containing information about resource status code, HTTP response headers.
4. It uses TCP connection for sending and receive on data on the web and before the request is send to the server there is 3 -way TCP handshake required to establish a connection to the server.
5. The default port for HTTP is 80. Ports are used to identity process or service on remote or local machine. It is logical path or communication channel for exchanging information with different server and machines over the internet.

HTTP Methods

HTTP Method is type of request or operation that is to be performed on resource requested by the client executed by the web server. The type of request made by the client is called the HTTP verb of the request. The verb indicates the action to be performed on the resource. There are mainly 6 request methods used on internet.

1. GET – It used to retrieve information or request for the resource from the requesting web server. The input parameters are in GET request which is used to get input from user in html document and process it to php script for storing in the server.
2. POST – It is used for uploading files and data to the remote server. The post request is used to submit form, files, data.
3. OPTIONS – This method is used to display all the available methods for requesting the resource on the server.
4. HEAD – It is similar to GET but doesn't retrieve message content from the http response.
5. TRACE – It is used for network diagnostics and troubleshooting, if the request fails.
6. DELETE – It is used to delete resource or file on the server. It is the most dangerous request as it could delete the files or data on the server.

HTTP Request & Response Format

Whenever a user makes a request for resource form the server there is certain piece of information that is send by the user such as HTTP Verb, HTTP Headers, HTTP Message Body to the web server. The web server analyses the request and process it according to HTTP Standard Request Format. The HTTP request consist of following parts:

- HTTP Verb

- HTTP Request Headers
- HTTP Message Body

Points to Note

- /r- It represents carrier return which is used for requesting a web server to provide access to resource and returning the content or webpage through the same request.
- /n: It represents the next line
- After every request line there is a space between the request lines and the headers.
- Format of HTTP Request: HTTP VERB/Resource Path/HTTP/Version

E.g. GET/ login.php? HTTP/1.1.

- HTTP Message Body contains data or information about the request being. It is empty or blank.

HTTP Request Headers

The HTTP Header fields are components of the header section of the request and response messages in the Hypertext Transfer Protocol (HTTP). They contain defining parameters and client, server to pass additional information with request or the response. The HTTP headers contain name followed by ':', then it is value. The custom headers are set by adding prefix 'X'. It contains information about the resource to be fetched or client itself. The following are some HTTP Headers Field Values:

- Content Length
- Content Type
- Content Encoding
- Connection
- Keep-Alive
- WWW-Authenticate
- Authorization
- Cache-Control
- Set-Cookie
- Origin
- User-Agent
- Cross-Origin Policy
- Content-Security Policy (CSP)

HTTP Request

HTTP-Request Line-GET /hello.html HTTP/1.1

HTTP Request Headers- User-Agent: Mozilla/4.0 (compatible; MSIE5.01;

Windows NT)

Host: www.xyz.com

Accept-Language: en-us

Accept-Encoding: gzip, deflate

Connection: Keep-Alive

HTTP Response

After receiving and interpreting a request message, a server responds with an HTTP response message:

- A Status-line
- Zero or more header (General | Response| Entity) fields followed by CRLF
- An empty line indicating the end of the header fields
- Optionally a message-body

Message Status-Line

A Status-Line consists of the protocol version followed by a numeric status code and its associated textual phrase. The elements are separated by space SP characters.

```
Status-Line = HTTP-Version SP Status-Code SP
Reason-Phrase CRLF
HTTP Version
A server supporting HTTP version 1.1 will return
the following version information:
HTTP-Version = HTTP/1.1
```

Status Code

The Status-Code element is a 3-digit integer where first digit of the Status-Code defines the class of response and the last two digits do not have any categorization role. There are 5 values for the first digit:

Code and Description
• 1xx: Informational: It means the request was received and the process is continuing.
• 2xx: Success: It means the action was successfully received, understood, and accepted.
• 3xx: Redirection: It means further action must be taken in order to complete the request.
• 4xx: Client Error: It means the request contains incorrect syntax or cannot be fulfilled.
• 5xx: Server Error: It means the server failed to fulfil an apparently valid request.

HTTP status codes are extensible and HTTP applications are not required to understand the meaning of all registered status codes.

HTTP Response Headers

```
HTTP/1.1 200 OK
Date: Mon 8 April 2019 12:28:53 GMT
Server: Apache/2.2.14 (Win32)
Last-Modified: Mon 8 April 2019 19:15:56 GMT
Content-Length: 89
Content-Type: text/html
Connection: Closed
```

HTTP Response Message Body

```
<html>
<body>
<h1>Hello, World! </h1>
</body>
</html>
```

HTTPS

HTTPS stands for Hypertext Transfer Protocol Secure, is an extension of HTTP which is used for secure communication over computer network. The main feature of HTTPS is providing an additional TLS/SSL support over HTTP. The HTTPS enables secure communication by providing encryption mechanism between user and Web Server. The HTTPS encrypts the content in the packet using SSL (Secure Socket Layer or Transport Layer Security) to avoid intercepting of the messages over network. The most important point to remember that HTTPS works with a Certificate Authority which validates Server Identity over the internet. An HTTP establishes an encrypted link over the HTTP using a digitally signed document which is verified by an organisation or CA and document signed by the CA is called Digital Certificate. A digital Certificate uses a standard of X.509 to establish a valid certificate and which is provided to Web Server by the CA after verifying it identify by an Registration Authority (RA). The party is given a certificate, they can view the credential, inspect the public key, use it to verify public key. The RA is an entity positioned between client and CA that is used to support CA before the digital Certificate is provided. The RA verifies user identity, accept responses. The HTTPS communication is started when 4-way Handshake between client and server is completed in order to start communication and the data is encrypted during the transaction. The following are the steps that is performed during handshake process.

Diagram HTTPS 4-way Handshake

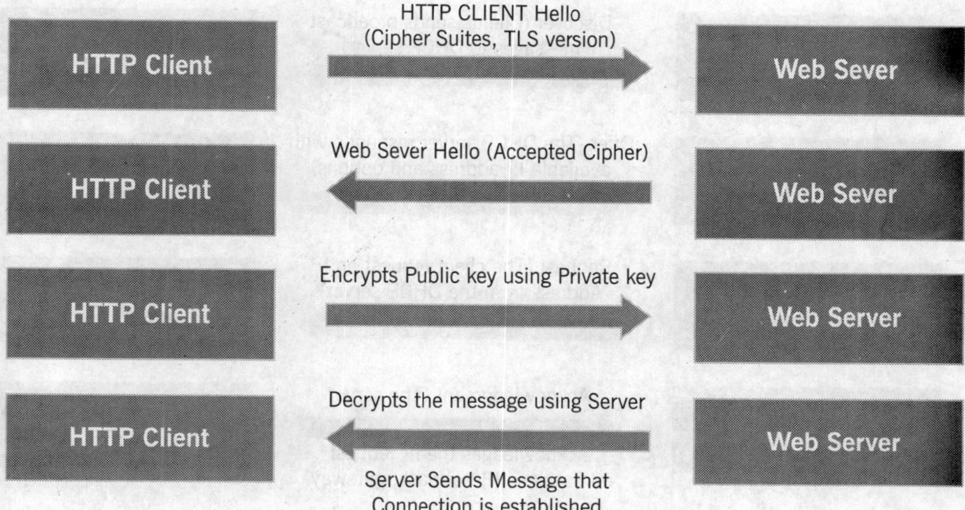

KEY NOTE

Key differences between HTTP & HTTPS

HTTP	HTTPS
Data transmitted is Unencrypted or in plain-text.	Data transmitted is Encrypted or in some form of cipher-text.
There is no SSL present in HTTP.	The SSL layer maintains secure communication
Less Secure in comparison to HTTPS.	Highly Secure in comparison to HTTP.
Stateless Protocol	Stateful Protocol because it uses cookies
Default Port 80	Default Port 443

Dynamic Host Configuration Protocol (DHCP)

The DHCP is a network management protocol used for dynamically assigning IP address to host on the computer network for communication between different host using IP. The DHCP has automatic IP addressing scheme and administration as we manually need not to be configure the devices in order, it assign IP address to every device on the network. The main function, it is assigns IP address and retrieve the Public IP address from Internet Service Provider (ISP). It runs on application layer on TCP/IP stack to dynamically assign IP addresses to DHCP clients and to allocate TCP/IP configuration information to DHCP clients. This includes subnet mask information, default gateway IP addresses and domain name system (DNS) addresses. DHCP uses default port 67. The DHCP is client-server protocol where server manages the IP address or pool of IP Address and parameters related to client information.

DHCP Handshake Diagram

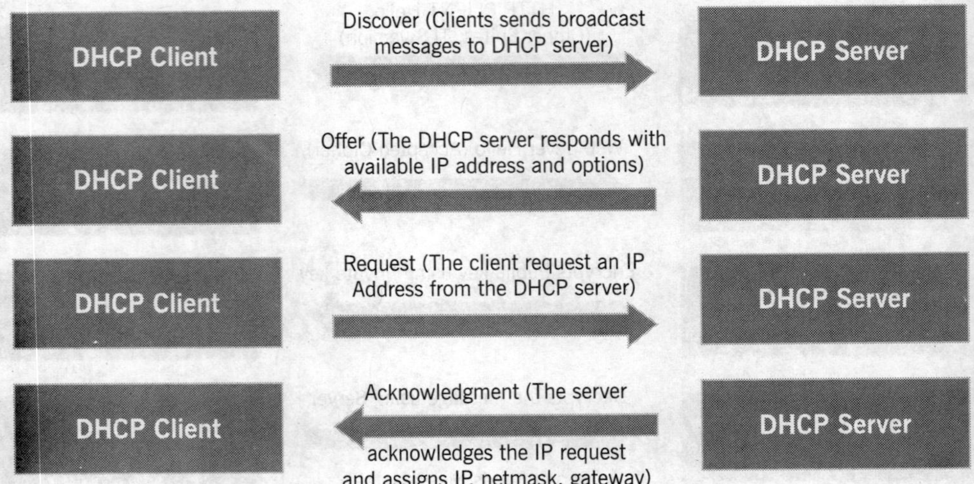

Telnet

The telnet utility is used for providing a text-based terminal on the remote systems or server and help us to establish a connection on port to different machine or computer. It is used for remote administration and network diagnostics purposes by network engineers. TELNET is a general protocol, meant to support logging in from almost any type of terminal to almost any type of computer.

- It allows a user at one site to establish a TCP connection to a login server or terminal server at another site.
- A TELNET server generally listens on TCP Port 23.
- Telnet even predates internetworking and the modern IP packet and TCP transport layers.
- The Telnet protocol provides a standardized interface, through which a program on one host (the Telnet client) may access the resources of another host (the Telnet server) as though the client were a local terminal connected to the server.
- For example, a user on a workstation on a LAN may connect to a host attached to the LAN as though the workstation were a terminal attached directly to the host. Of course, Telnet may be used across WANs as well as LANs.
- Most Telnet implementations do not provide you with graphics capabilities.

Remote Desktop Protocol (RDP)

Remote desktop protocol (*RDP*) is a secure network communications protocol designed for remote management, as well as for remote access to virtual desktops, applications and an *RDP* terminal server. *RDP* allows network administrators to remotely diagnose and resolve problems individual subscribers encounter. The RDP protocol is a proprietary protocol developed by Microsoft, which provides a user with a graphical interface to connect to another computer over a network connection. The user employs RDP client software for this purpose, while the other computer must run RDP server software. It runs on default Port 3389.

File Transfer Protocol (FTP)

The file transfer protocol allows users to transfer share files, directories between client-server over computer network. It is built on client-server architecture and works on control and data connections between the client and the server. FTP promotes sharing of files via remote computers with reliable and efficient data transfer. Files can be transferred between two computers using FTP software. The user's computer is called the local host machine and is connected to the Internet. The second machine, called the remote host, is also running FTP software and connected to the Internet. The local host machine connects to the remote host's IP address. The user would enter a username/password (or use anonymously). FTP software may have GUI, allowing users to drag and drop files between the remote and local host. If not, a series of FTP Commands are used for logging in to the remote host and transfer files between the machines. The default Port used for FTP is 21 called command port and Port 20 is used for controlling and communication with FTP servers also known as data port.

Server Message Block (SMB)

Server Message Block (SMB) is a service intended to provide shared access to files, serial ports, printers, and communications between nodes on a network. TCP port 445 you can directly access the TCP/IP MS Networking without the help of a NetBIOS layer. You can only get this service in recent versions of Windows, such as Windows2K/XP. File sharing in Windows2K/XP can be done only by using Server Message Block (SMB) protocol. You can also run SMB directly over TCP/IP in Windows 2K/XP without using the help of extra layer of NetBT. The SMB service using TCP protocol for giving access to shares and resources.

NetBIOS

NetBIOS stands for Network Basic Input Output System. It was developed by Syntek in association with IBM. NetBIOS is used to enumerate NetBIOS name, services, users, workgroup, domain information about the remote computer. A NetBIOS was originally developed as Application Programming Interface (API) to facilitate LAN resources. The

NetBIOS name is a unique 16 ASCII character string used to identify the network devices over TCP/IP; 15 characters are used for the device name and the 16th character is reserved for the service or name record type. If an attacker finds a Windows OS with port 139 open, he or she would be interested in checking what resources he or she can access, or view, on the remote system. However, to enumerate the NetBIOS names, the remote system must have enabled file and printer sharing. Using these techniques, the attacker can launch two types of attacks on a remote computer that has NetBIOS. The attacker can choose to read/write to a remote computer system, depending on the availability of shares, or launch a denial-of-service. NetBIOS name resolution is not supported by Microsoft for Internet Protocol Version 6(IPv6).

NETBIOS NAME LIST

NAME	NETBIOS CODE	TYPE	Information Obtained
Hostname	<00>	UNIQUE	Hostname
Domain Name	<00>	GROUP	Domain Name
Hostname	<03>	UNIQUE	Messenger Services running for the host
User	<03>	UNIQUE	Messenger services running for users that is logged-in
Hostname	<20>	UNIQUE	File Server Service Running
Domain	<1D>	GROUP	Master Browser Name for subnet
Domain	<1B>	UNIQUE	Domain Master Browser Name

Diagrammatic Representation of NetBIOS

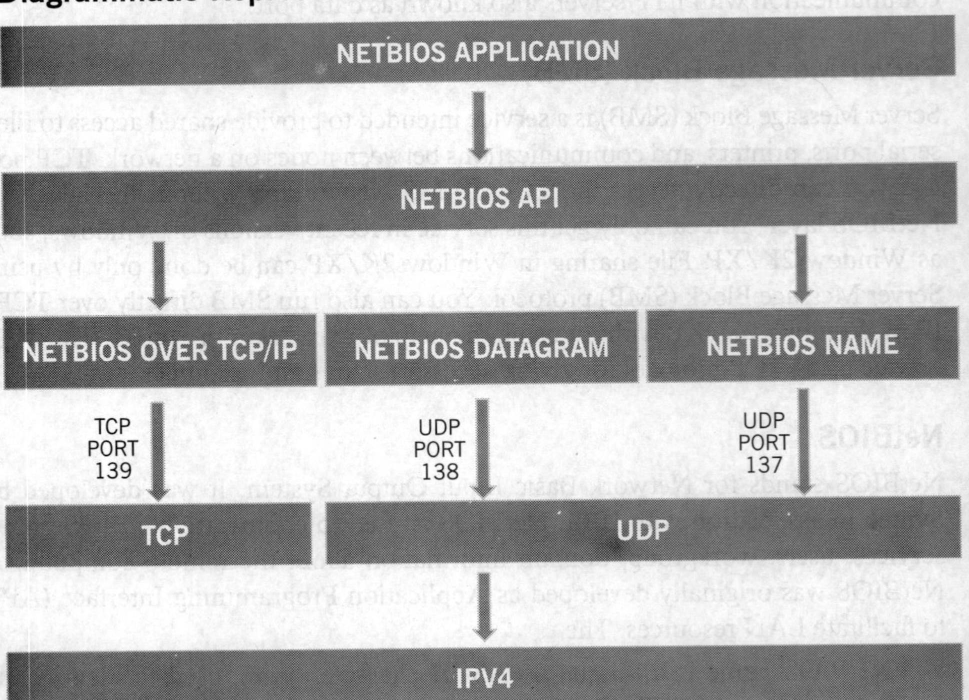

DOMAIN NAME SYSTEM (DNS)

DNS stands for Domain Name System, it is the used for resolving Hostname to IP Address to view and give access to a resource on the internet. The DNS has a fixed hierarchy which is used for name resolution and works on UDP Port 53. The client sends a request to local DNS resolver or DNS of ISP which has IP address of the root server encoded within itself. The resolver sends the request to root server asking the IP Address on any xy.com and the server replies with an answer of IP Address of a Top-level Domain inquiring about the IP of xy.com. Each DNS request has transaction id to track request and response associated with client-DNS Servers.

DOMAIN NAME SYNTAX

Protocol: Host. Sub-domain. Domain. TLD.

KEY NOTE

- The Protocol determines that the set of rules used for requesting a resource from the Web Server generally HTTP, HTTPS.
- The rightmost (.) is determined as the root domain.
- Then next to it is Top-level Domain, storing information about commercial and government domains such as .com, .net, .au etc.
- The third part is Domain which is actual the name of the website, which is officially registered by registering the Authority of the website.
- The Sub-Domain is child of parent domain.
- Each label can have maximum of 63 characters and maximum length of entire domain name cannot be greater than 253 characters.
- Labels can have lower-case letters, digits, hyphens.

DNS Servers

- Authoritative Server- Serves for Zones it is responsible for and master source for DNS zone. A DNS zone portion of DNS namespace that have administrative responsibility for serving and managing records. The TLD servers also has authoritative that contain information about secondary domain servers, and there are 13 root name servers that contains information about TLD Servers. Every domain almost 2 authoritative for security concern.
- Caching Server- Recursively lookup for DNS records not authoritative for and is used for caching DNS information until TTL expires.

DNS Records

- A - stores IPV4 Address
- AAA - stores IPV6 Address

- CNAME - Canonical Name Alias
- MX - Mail Servers
- NS - Name Server
- SRV - Service locator
- TXT - Text Pseudo Records
- PTR - Reverse IP Lookup
- SOA - Start of Authority
- SPF - Sender Policy
- AXFR - Authoritative zone transfer
- IXFR - Incremental zone transfer

Working of DNS

- A user request for xyz.com and request is sent to host file of the computer where there this lookup of the domain and if the domain is available than the website is loaded.
- If the domain is not found, the OS sends it to DNS resolver which contains a local hierarchy of database values containing available domains that ISP can serve.
- The ISP lookups in local Database and checks if that domain is found then is loaded or else processed to root server(.)
- The query is asked about xyz.com IP address but the root server does not know it, but knows the IP of TLD Serves which contains info about .com domain.
- The request further goes to TLD and processed to asked the same query but the TLD Servers is not aware xyz.com but knows the IP address of name server responsible for handling and loading the website.
- Finally, the name server contains information about xyz.com and sends the information to DNS resolver for caching so that next time same query does not need to perform the complete lookup.
- The website is cached and displayed on the web browser with xyz.com domain and also if there is any sub domain that is processed by the name server as it contains domain/sub domain related information about the website as it is an authoritative server which has rights to manage and process domain related information.

Summary

In this chapter, we have looked at basic concepts and working of networking components. We have learned about OSI Model, TCP/IP Model and their implementation. IP Address topics covered in this chapter are highly important and recommended to learn properly. There are various protocols which are covered in this chapter such as TCP, UDP, HTTP, HTTPS, DNS, etc. In the next chapter, we will look at Virtualization Technology and how to set our Kali Linux Penetration Testing Lab and also, we will learn to use Linux Command Line.

4 Virtualization & Working with Linux Virtual Machine (VM)

Module Outlines

- Introduction to Virtualization
- Virtualization Tools & Technologies
- Setting up & working with Virtual Machine
- Installing Kali Linux
- Getting Started with Linux Command Line
- Basic Commands
- Linux Package Managers

Virtualization, as we discussed already in the previous chapter, is a great technology which allows us to create multiple virtual copies of environments (like Operating Systems) on a single physical device. It is a basic definition of virtualization, but it is expanded beyond this.

Virtualization is a widely used, appreciated and useful technology which reduced the resource wastage, improved security and provided better management of a resource. Let's understand this concept with some real-life scenario and then we will look at the technicality of virtualization.

Consider, a two-storey house as a resource, at present only ground floor is occupied and the rest of the building is of no use. Now, if we rent the remaining storey or use them for guest hosting (something like AirBnb or Paying Guest concept), we can utilize the two-storey without investing in another building and also it is easier for the owner to manage the side business effectively and security of the house is also maintained. This type of concept can also be seen in computing resources as well.

Consider, we have a computing system having 12GBs of RAM, 2 TBs of disk space and other good specification and currently running on Windows Operating System & have enough free resources. Now, there is an urgent requirement of running Linux Operating System which requires to either purchase a new system or replace it with windows system. Both are costly in terms of either money or time consumption & in the second case what if we need both the Windows &

Linux environment parallelly. Now, through the virtualization technology, we can use the free resource of the existing system to install Linux Operating System and perform desired task. It will not only save cost but also reduce resource wastage and improve the security of the system.

The above example gives a broader picture to virtualization and tells us it's simple renting the available space in existing resource to some other process for better and optimized resource sharing, smooth processing and improved security.

Virtualization refers to create a virtual (imaginary) instance of some computing resource like an operating system, server, network or an application. It is used to achieve simultaneous and parallel processing of multiple instances.

The Hypervisor is a software entity which is used to directly connect and interact with the physical system and split it to distinct and secure environments, called as **Virtual Machines (VMs).**

The original machine with the Hypervisor is known as **Host Machines** & the Virtual Machines created are known as **Guest Machines.**

There are various types of virtualization, like:

1. Operating System Virtualization
2. Server Virtualization
3. Desktop Virtualization
4. Data Virtualization
5. Network Virtualization

Virtual Machine is a platform used to achieve the concept of virtualization. There are following benefits of using virtual machine:

1. Proper Resource Utilization
2. Reduce Cost & Save Money
3. Centralized Control
4. Management of Data Centre is simplified
5. Easy Error & Disaster Recovery
6. Enhanced Security
7. Better IT Productivity

There are some popular tools used for creating virtual machine(s):

1. VMware Workstation/Player
2. Oracle Virtual Box (Free & Open Source)
3. Parallel Desktop
4. Hyper – V

Throughout this book, we will work on VMware Workstation and further in this chapter, we will look how to work with VMware Workstation and install a Linux Virtual Machine and learn the required concepts of Linux Operating System.

Installing VMware Workstation

1. Visit www.vmware.com and download an evaluation copy of VMware Workstation.
2. Open Installation Package and Install VMware Workstation.
3. If you have purchased tool, validate and activate the evaluation copy.

Creating Kali Linux Virtual Machine

Kali Linux is a Debian Linux Distribution based operating system and is one of the most popular operating system used among security professionals, researchers and hackers. Kali contains a rich set of pre-installed and configured tools and libraries that are most popular and widely used for performing various attacks. Kali can be considered as the Swiss Army Knife among all other Hacking Operating Systems. There are various other Operating Systems which are widely used like **Parrot Security OS, BlackArch, BackBox, Pentoo, BugTraq, Samurai Web Testing Framework, etc.**

1. Visit www.kali.org and download Kali Linux ISO according to your system architecture (we will be using 64-bit image).
2. Open VMware Workstation Pro and navigate to **Create New Virtual Machine** option.
3. Select Typical > Installer Disc Image File and Provide **Path of Kali Linux ISO** that you downloaded > Select **Linux** as **Guest Operating System** and **Version** as **Ubuntu 64-bit** (select ubuntu 32-bit, if your system is 32-bit)
4. Provide **Virtual Machine Name & Location.**
5. Provide **Maximum Disk Size** (60 GB is preferred.)
6. Finish and on the right side you will notice under **My Computers,** your VM Name will appear.
7. Click on the **Virtual Machine Name** & click on **Power on this Virtual Machine** & your virtual machine will start.

Installing Kali Linux

1. Boot (turn on) Kali Linux VM and select Graphical Install. (please note that Live Mode is for Plug and Play, it will not store any of the work and is volatile by default.)

```
Install
Graphical install
Install with speech synthesis
```

2. Choose **English** Language. (or any other according to your preference, this book follows English Language) and continue.

3. Select your Country and continue.
4. Select **American English** as keymap. (you may select other according to your language preference. Keymap represents your keyboard layout *i.e.* on which keystroke, what will be reflected).
5. Provide Hostname. (The hostname is a single word that identifies your system on the network)
6. Provide Domain (If you are not aware what to provide, you can **leave this field empty and continue).**
7. Set Root Password (you will require this to login) and Enter Full Name of the User.
8. Partitioning Step is little tricky and most of the users for the first time, end up doing it wrong and wipe their Windows partition. Since we are using it in VM mode, we needn't to provide about this. **Simply choose Guided – use entire disk.**

Partitioning method:

Guided - use entire disk
Guided - use entire disk and set up LVM
Guided - use entire disk and set up encrypted LVM
Manual

9. In partitioning scheme, select as per highlighted in screenshot.

Partitioning scheme:

All files in one partition (recommended for new users)
Separate /home partition
Separate /home, /var, and /tmp partitions

10. At last, Finish partitioning and continue to install the system (It might take time depending upon the resources allocated to VM).
11. Install the Grub and your Kali VM is ready to hunt.

Working with Terminal (CLI) and Basic Commands & Configurations

Terminal or Shell is the Command Line Interface or you may refer it as heart/ core of the Linux and most popular tool for the security professionals. There are various types of shells like:

- Bash – Bourne Again Shell
- Csh/TCsh – C Shell
- Zsh – Z Shell
- Ksh – Korn Shell

Bourne Again Shell (Bash) is one of the popular Linux shells.

A terminal is available in Kali Linux, and throughout this book, we will interact with terminal many times. It is essential to get your hands dirty with terminal and have comfort working on CLI environment. There are several pros of working with command lines, like:

1. Attackers rarely have access to GUI, they access the Command Line in most of the cases, that's why it's the best practice to have your hands dirty on Command Line.
2. Command Injection is one of the common vulnerabilities and it requires CLI Knowledge.
3. Command line is faster than most of the GUI Application because the processing involved in initializing graphical vectors is eliminated.
4. Command line can be Automated & Scripted Easily.

Let's start exploring and playing around terminal in Kali Linux. For this **Turn on and Login to your VM.**

There are various methods, from where you can access and open Kali Linux Terminal:

1. Click Black Icon with $ sign on Quick Access Tray in the Left side.

2. Press Window Key and search Terminal.

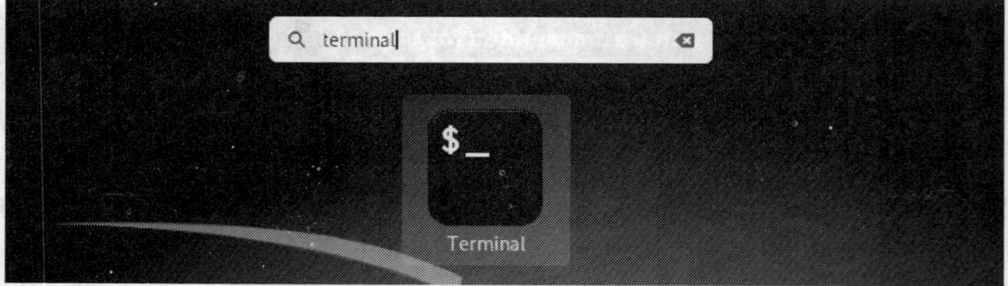

3. Click on Application in Top Bar and Select Terminal under Favourite section.

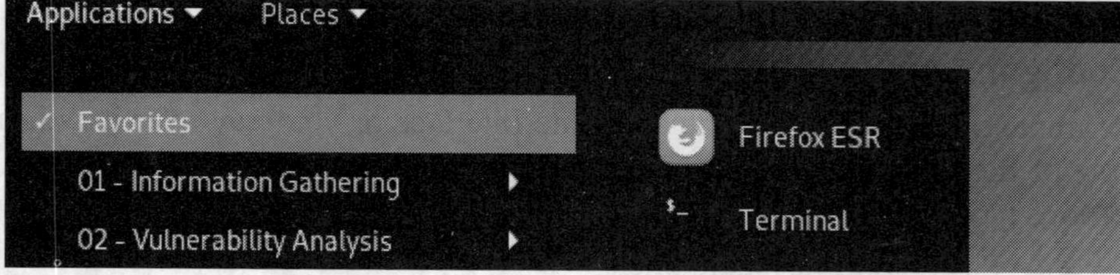

4. The very first step you need to do after installing your kali linux system is to check for updates and install latest dependencies, if any. To perform this, follow the steps :
    1. Open terminal.

2. Type following command

```
sudo apt-get update && apt-get upgrade
```

3. Output will be like

```
root@kali:~# sudo apt-get update && apt-get
upgrade
Hit:1 https://ftp.acc.umu.se/mirror/kali.org/kali
kali-rolling InRelease
```

Reading package lists... Done

Reading package lists... Done

Building dependency tree

```
<end of command>
```

This command will update kali to latest version.

Basic Commands

1. man – it is used to check manual of any tool.

```
man <command_name>
root@kali:~# man ls
```

```
LS(1)                          User Commands                          LS(1)

NAME
       ls - list directory contents

SYNOPSIS
       ls [OPTION]... [FILE]...

DESCRIPTION
       List  information  about the FILEs (the current directory by default). Sort entries alphabeti-
       cally if none of -cftuvSUX nor --sort is specified.

       Mandatory arguments to long options are mandatory for short options too.

       -a, --all
              do not ignore entries starting with .

       -A, --almost-all
              do not list implied . and ..

       --author
              with -l, print the author of each file
```

2. **ls** – used to list items present in the directory.

```
root@kali:~# ls
Desktop   Downloads   index.html   Music
Public   Templates   Videos
```

3. **cd** – used to change directory from one to another.

```
root@kali:~# cd Desktop
root@kali:~/Desktop#
```

using this command, from root directory we entered into **Desktop Directory**.

4. **pwd** – prints working directory

```
root@kali:~/Desktop# pwd
/root/Desktop
```

5. **mkdir & rmdir** – use to make and remove directories respectively.

```
root@kali:~/Desktop# mkdir new
root@kali:~/Desktop# ls
latesttools  mount-shared-folders  new
(a directory named new is created)
root@kali:~/Desktop# rmdir new
root@kali:~/Desktop# ls
latesttools  mount-shared-folders
(a directory named new is removed)
```

6. **ps** – displays a list of running processes.

```
root@kali:~/Desktop# ps
PID TTY          TIME CMD
2013 pts/0    00:00:00 bash
2395 pts/0    00:00:00 ps
```

7. **chmod** – changes the access permissions of a file or directory.

```
root@kali:~/Desktop# chmod a+x abc.txt
```

8. **ifconfig** – displays the network related information.

```
root@kali:~# ifconfig
eth0: flags=4163<UP,BROADCAST,RUNNING,MULTICAST>
mtu 1500
        inet 192.168.121.137  netmask
255.255.255.0  broadcast 192.168.121.255
        inet6 fe80::20c:29ff:fec7:c345  prefixlen
64  scopeid 0x20<link>
lo: flags=73<UP,LOOPBACK,RUNNING>  mtu 65536
        inet 127.0.0.1  netmask 255.0.0.0
        inet6 ::1  prefixlen 128  scopeid
0x10<host>
<end of command>
```

9. **netstat** – displays the TCP & UDP connection information.

```
root@kali:~# netstat
Active Internet connections (w/o servers)
Proto Recv-Q Send-Q Local Address           Foreign
Address       State
Active UNIX domain sockets (w/o servers)
Proto RefCnt Flags       Type       State
I-Node   Path
unix  2      [ ]         DGRAM
24121    /run/user/0/systemd/notify
unix  3      [ ]         DGRAM
12398    /run/systemd/notify
```

```
unix  15      [ ]         DGRAM
12418    /run/systemd/journal/dev-log
unix  2       [ ]         DGRAM
12423    /run/systemd/journal/syslog
<end of command>
```

10. ping – sends ICMP Echo request to target network host.

```
root@kali:~# ping 127.0.0.1
PING 127.0.0.1 (127.0.0.1) 56(84) bytes of data.
64 bytes from 127.0.0.1: icmp_seq=1 ttl=64
time=0.032 ms
64 bytes from 127.0.0.1: icmp_seq=2 ttl=64
time=0.071 ms
^C
--- 127.0.0.1 ping statistics ---
3 packets transmitted, 3 received, 0% packet loss,
time 37ms
rtt min/avg/max/mdev = 0.027/0.043/0.071/0.020 ms
<end of command>
```

Special Characters and Wildcards

Character	Usage
/	Used to separate directory
\	It is an escape character used for referencing
.	Represents Current Directory. It can be used along with **cd** to jump into Current Directory.
..	Represents Parent Directory. It can be used along with **cd** to jump into Parent Directory.
~	Represents user's Home Directory. It can be used along with **cd** to jump into Home Directory
&	Executes a command in background.
;	Command separator. It can be used to run multiple commands.
&&	Command separator. (based on AND condition)
||	Command separator. (based on OR condition)
*	Wildcard used to **Select All** files with a specific pattern.
[]	Used to provide a range of values.

Some Examples

```
Ex - 1:  Directory Separator (/)
         root@kali:~# cd Desktop/latesttools/
Ex - 2:  Parent Directory (..)
```

```
              root@kali:~/Desktop/latesttools# cd ..
              root@kali:~/Desktop#
              (we jumped back to Desktop directory in
              this case.)
     Ex - 3:  Home Directory (~)
              root@kali:~/Desktop# cd ~
              root@kali:~#
              (we jumped back to Home directory in this
              case.)
     Ex - 4:  Command Separator (;)
              root@kali:~# cd Desktop; cd latesttools
              root@kali:~/Desktop/latesttools#
```

Package Managers

Packages in the Linux are the bundle of software or services which can be used to install or update a new or existing service. For example, if you want to use python3 in Linux but assume it's not installed, now in this case either you have to download the linux installation files and do the long manual process or simply you can locate the package name of the python3 for your linux distribution and install from either CLI or GUI with the help of package managers. Most Linux Distributions uses some sort of management system to speed up the installation process and make it less error prone, ie. **Package Manager.**

Kali Linux is a Debian based linux distribution which uses **APT** (Advance Packaging Tool) as package manager.

Example

```
sudo apt-get install python3
```

There are many other concepts in Linux to explore. To smoothly learn from this book, we have looked at enough resources. If you are willing to learn Linux in more depth, you can refer to following online resources –

```
http://linuxcommand.org/
https://github.com/aleksandar-todorovic/awesome-
linux
https://www.linux.org
```

Summary

In this chapter, we explore virtualization technology and various tools used for achieving virtualization. We installed VMware as a tool for virtualization & installed Kali Linux Operating System. We learned about various command line tools which are required throughout & concept of package managers in Linux. Further in the next chapter, we will look at the formal introduction to information gathering.

PART-2

INFORMATION GATHERING & OPEN SOURCE INTELLIGENCE

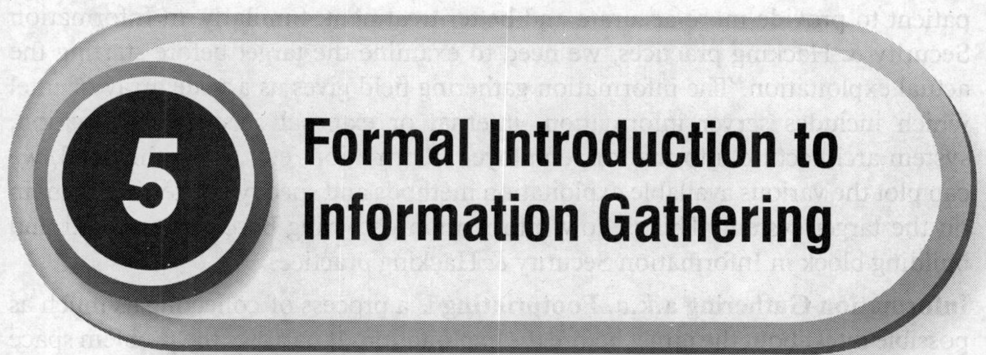

5 Formal Introduction to Information Gathering

Module Outlines

- Introduction to Information Gathering
- What to Expect from Information Gathering?
- Types of Information Gathering

Information is essential in the 21st century. With constant digitization and evolution of the internet, data storage, integrity and security are major concerns. We have already discussed information and information intelligence in initial chapters of part-1 and looked at various requirements to start with information security.

This part focus on various information gathering and open source intelligence-based tactics, methodologies and tools required for the information gathering from various resources. There are many practices included along with use case scenarios and some example of **when to use what** *i.e.* in which scenario which tool or technique is perfect to work with. In this section, we will mainly focus on the tools which are either accessible online, available without a paid license & is free and many other laymen to intermediate tools. Please notice that you will need a high-speed active internet connection to smoothly run and practice tools. This chapter will give you a formal introduction and a wide scope about information gathering. Let's dive deep into crawling various information sources and perform some intel gathering.

Information Gathering

Information Gathering is an art, tool, technique or method of studying various resources for information to extract useful intel. The sources can be social media, company profile, personal contacts, referrals or come in any other electronic and non-electronic form.

Information Gathering practices is one of the building steps in Information Security lifecycle. Before testing any system or service, a thorough study and analysis are required to know about it. Just like, for medical diagnosis, the doctor asks for all the symptoms, previous history and other relevant things and predict & prescribe course of treatment. The questions asked are to gather information about patient to provide more accurate and better treatment. Similarly, in Information Security & Hacking practices, we need to examine the target before starting the actual exploitation. The information gathering field gives us a wide array of intel which includes server information, internal or external security information, system architecture information, employee information, etc. Using this intel, we can plot the various available exploitation methods and specify our testing domain on the target system. This is how information gathering becomes essential and building block in Information Security & Hacking practices.

Information Gathering a.k.a. Footprinting is a process of collecting as much as possible intel about the target before the exploitation. It narrows the problem space and helps in identifying specific domains for exploitation.

Information Gathering can be used to identify internal or external physical and logical security posture of the target and allows identifying well known and most commonly appearing vulnerabilities according to the target system's technology.

In some cases, the target system is new to us and we are not aware of any single detail. In this case, it is very important to examine and identify the technologies running on the target system or the technologies which are used to build the target system so that specific and optimal attacks can be performed. Information Gathering helps identifying the technologies running or used in the target system.

Information Gathering often becomes the most crucial part in any hacking process because it involves specifying attack vectors, vulnerabilities, the overall posture of the target system and is the base for further decision making & exploitation.

Information Gathering – What to Expect

Information Gathering is not limited to the electronic medium, even in daily life we perform a lot of information gathering (give a though, how we do it in daily life and try to relate it.) and are unaware of it. If we know the tactics and methods, we can improve the information gathering skills both in the electronic and non-electronic medium. Let's look at what information gathering can get us in most of the scenarios.

The various intel gathered can be:

1. Internet Protocol (IP) Address
2. DNS Information
3. Mail Server Information
4. HTTP/HTTPS Protocol Information
5. Ports & Protocol Information
6. Technologies Used
7. TCP & UDP Service(s) Information
8. Subdomain & Active Directory Information
9. Network Blocks & VPN Points

10. Intrusion Detection System Information
11. Firewall Information
12. User & Group Information
13. System Architecture Information
14. Sensitive Information such as Passwords
15. Routing Tables
16. Employee Details
17. Internal Security Posture
18. External Security Posture
19. Physical Security & Infrastructure Information
20. Target for Social Engineering
21. Policies
22. Archives
23. Social Media & Private Information
24. Website Statistics & Analytics
25. IT Device Default Credentials
26. Link Extractions
27. Codebase through mirroring
28. Live Web Cams
29. Geo Location Tracking
30. Crawling Public Government Records
31. Fake News Detection

Moreover, the list is very long & we can expect many methods and useful intel from Information gathering which can simplify our whole process of hacking into a target system. Throughout this book, we will look at various tools and methods of gathering the intel including the mentioned above and some other as well.

It is important to understand the cruciality of the information because even a little single piece of information help make a change in decision or achieve a decision. It is must to practice all the methods and tools on a regular basis so that you can master them and it is essential.

Types of Information Gathering

Information Gathering is classified into two broad categories, which are:

1. Active Information Gathering
2. Passive Information Gathering

Active Information Gathering

Active Information Gathering involves gathering intel through various resources by **Actively or Directly Interacting** with the target. It is generally considered as one to one or target – attacker information gathering cycle. For example, performing query directory on the target's web application to gather information. We will look at various Active Information Gathering methods in further chapters.

Passive Information Gathering

Passive Information Gathering involves gathering intel through various resources by **Indirectly Interacting or Without Interacting** with the target or. It is generally considered as no connection between target and tester. For example, performing query on the social media or performing open source intelligence to gather information about target system. We will look at various Active Information Gathering methods in further chapters.

We will now look at various tools, techniques and methodologies of performing information gathering through online available tools, resources and passive information gathering methods.

Summary

In this chapter, we just formally looked at what information gathering is and what is its scope. We have looked at what kind of information can be gathered and used in various cases. There are two types of information gathering which we have covered. In the next chapter, we will look at Information Gathering Tools & Methodologies.

6 Information Gathering Tools & Methodologies

Module Outlines

- Information Gathering through common methods
- Information Gathering involving use of E-Media
- Information Gathering using Online Tools

Information Gathering Methodologies and Techniques are widely used for the intel gathering. It is essential to know about a variety of available options and have knowledge of when to use what method. In this chapter, we will explore a wide array of such methods.

Information Gathering through common methods

1. **Dumpster Diving** – It is a method of searching for the critical document, piece of paper or anything useful in the dump or recycling area. Often, in a hurry, people tend to throw away documents having some important information without destroying it. If investigator finds it, it becomes a useful piece of information. We have often seen an example of dumpster diving in the Crime TV Shows or movies where investigation officers look for every single piece of information as evidence and getting partial burnt picture or documents might lead to a new direction in investigation.
2. **Shoulder Surfing** – One of the basic methods of breaching someone's privacy or accessing private information by physically interacting with someone and applying shoulder surfing. In shoulder surfing we observe a person typing or try to look into his activity with a sharp eye to guess the password or get to know, what's happening or what's going on with the target.
3. **Eavesdropping** – It is similar to Shoulder Surfing, and we try to gather some intel by spying or friendly keeping an eye on a person. We try to eavesdrop into a target's personal information.
4. **Social Engineering** – Social Engineering is the most powerful call of action and can be used to extract any information and is more effective than any tool. Social Engineering is widely popular as the Art of Human Exploitation.

It involves attacking emotions or human behaviour to gain the advantage of human vulnerabilities. Humans are widely vulnerable to many things, and if a sharp social engineer tries to populate the vulnerable point and take advantage of it, he can extract a wide variety of useful information.

5. **Contact Chaining** – This is a common method each of us uses in day to day life. If we are looking for some information about someone, we often at first place, try to ask our contacts or try to get some reference. Contact Chaining is nothing, but gathering the information about the target by using the contacts (personal or professional) and their referrals to establish a referential connection between target and attacker.

   For Example, Ram wants to gather information about Shiv but he has no direct contact with him. He asks his friend Vijay to look for Shiv's contact. Vijay tell him that shiv is his friend and provide basic details about Shiv. In this way, the contact chaining works.

6. Intel Gathering through Identity Theft – Identity Theft is a process where an attacker pretends to be someone else. We have often seen in movies when intelligence agency officers or agents fake their passports and become someone else to accomplish their mission. The same process is identity theft. Here we pretend to be someone else (someone with authority maybe) to gather as much as possible intel about the target.

   For example, calling at a company reception and pretending to be someone else, someone as a part of their company or as an authority to extract the information. Often employees due to fear of authority, they provide the information in a humble way and fall prey of this type of method.

   These are some of the common methods that you are probably using in your day to day life and are easy to remember & implement. There is no technicality in these methods and are simplest & evergreen but the practise is still required and recommended to improve the success rate in extracting the information. There might be some other common methods which you can generate by your own and practice. Further, we will look at some of the common technical methodologies which involve digital technology or electronic medium interactions.

Basic Methods of Information Gathering involving Electronic Medium Interactions

1. **Google** – Google is one of the widely used and popular search engine & a great tool for optimal information gathering. Nowadays, if we want to query anything, we simply ask google and get desired results, but this is just the basic usage of google as a search engine. We can search for the target on google and can get its various information like company profile, product range, contact details, employee information, leaked private information, market reputation and shares information and much more. It helps us to determine internal

and external company posture and further can be used to plot human based information gathering.

As a power user, we can query and ask google for a specific piece of information through the use of advance complex query, also known as, **Google Dorks.**

2. **Company Website** – If our target is an organizational body having an online presence (generally in the form of a website) or individual having employment at such organization, we can crawl the target's company website to gather information about it. Often the company website contains information such as employee details, public archives, contact details, product information and through applying advance methodologies, we can even get some private information stored on the server without proper security. That information might turn to be sensitive as well.

   While performing hacking, penetration testing or investigation, our aim is not always related to exploiting social media account, getting admin access or making it inaccessible. The aim depends according to the scope of the test and this scope is determined through Information Gathering and, in many cases, only information gathering and advanced scanning methods are alone sufficient in achieving our goals.

3. **Social Media Networks** – Social Media has become an essential part of the life and even large organizations use social media for their promotion, activity and engagement with a large pool of audience.

   Social Media is a great tool for information gathering, by thoroughly examining, we can predict the various patterns and trends followed by an organization or business entity, we can track the movements of a socially active person, and we can manipulate a person by social engineering through social media. Social Engineering through social media can be seen most effective in youths, where talking to someone pretending someone else (identity theft using fake accounts) and trying to manipulate (social engineering through gaining trust) to get a useful piece of information and sometimes it may be sensitive information as well.

4. **Wikipedia & Public Website** – Many Popular target's information can be gathered from Wikipedia and another public website which sometimes contains personal information of the target or maybe information leakage about a product or service.

5. **Location Information with Geo-Location Websites** – Geo-location-based websites such as Google Maps, Wikimapia, etc. can be used to determine the physical location of the target. Google Earth also provides 3D visuals and other information which can be relevant in many scenarios.

6. **Corporate Profiles** – Corporate profiles can be gathered about the target using websites like google finance, yahoo finance and job sites like LinkedIn, Monster, Indeed, etc.

These are some of the common methods to gather information interacting with technology. Now we will look at various tools available online and methods to gather structured and more accurate intel (information which provides us intellectual decision making and is extremely useful).

Information Gathering using Online Tools & Other Methodologies

1. **Netcraft – www.netcraft.com** – Netcraft provides internet security services including anti-fraud and anti-phishing services, application testing and PCI scanning. It also analyses many aspects of the internet, including the market share of web servers, operating systems, hosting providers and SSL certificate authorities. (according to netcraft website)

   It audits websites and stores a report database which can be utilized for gathering information about the target website. Follow the steps to check audit reports –

   1. Visit www.netcraft.com
   2. Input target website in What's the Site Running? Widget.

   What's that site running?

   Find out what technologies are powering any website:

   google.com →

   3. It will show the various results and we can modify the search results as well by modifying the left field having default value "site contains".

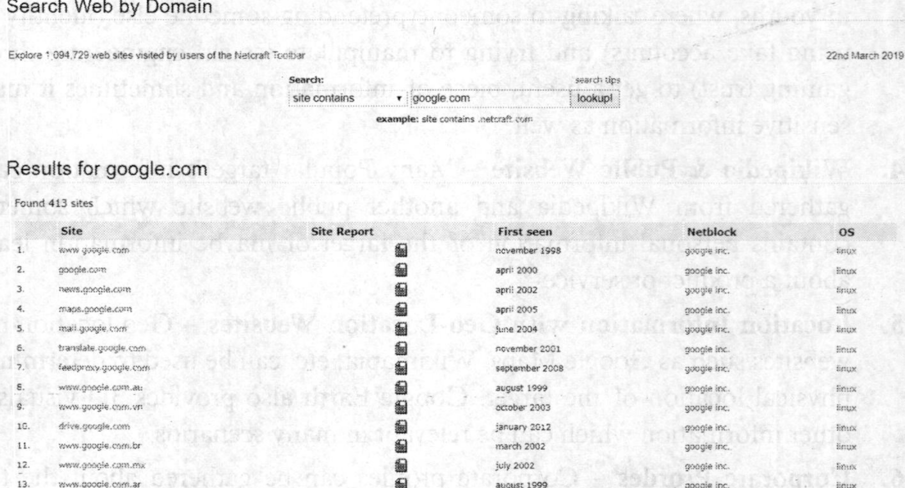

Search Web by Domain

Explore 1,094,729 web sites visited by users of the Netcraft Toolbar — 22nd March 2019

Search: site contains ▾ google.com lookup! (search tips)

example: site contains .netcraft.com

Results for google.com

Found 413 sites

	Site	Site Report	First seen	Netblock	OS
1.	www.google.com		november 1998	google inc.	linux
2.	google.com		april 2000	google inc.	linux
3.	news.google.com		april 2002	google inc.	linux
4.	maps.google.com		april 2005	google inc.	linux
5.	mail.google.com		june 2004	google inc.	linux
6.	translate.google.com		november 2001	google inc.	linux
7.	feedproxy.google.com		september 2008	google inc.	linux
8.	www.google.com.au		august 1999	google inc.	linux
9.	www.google.com.vn		october 2003	google inc.	linux
10.	drive.google.com		january 2012	google inc.	linux
11.	www.google.com.br		march 2002	google inc.	linux
12.	www.google.com.mx		july 2002	google inc.	linux
13.	www.google.com.ar		august 1999	google inc.	linux

   4. Click on the report icon in Site Report column of the desired result.
   5. It will open the report and we can gather following useful information –

a. IP Address (v4 & v6)

b. Nameserver & DNS Information

c. Hosting History

d. Sender Policy Framework, DMARC & Web Trackers

e. Site Technologies – Server Side, Client Side, Scripting Frameworks, Character Encoding, Privacy Management and Web Browser Targeting, etc.

Along with the various information, their description is written which will give an understanding about the service.

It is also useful to gather information of subdomains. For example, news. google.com

2. **Google Dorks** – As we discussed earlier in this chapter, Google dorks are the advance complex queries or regular expression (regex) based queries to filter results and narrow search space. It is very useful and essential. There are many google dorks, and a few important and useful dorks are –

   a. site: it limits the search to a specific website only. In some scenarios, we need to look for a string or query to be present in the specific domain only but google searches it everywhere, this dork can be useful in such case.

   For example: site:cybersquareinfo.com "Digital"

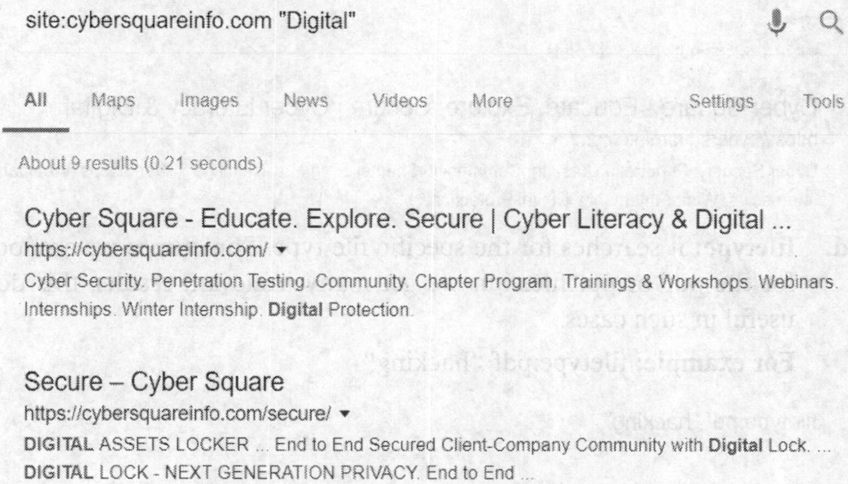

   b. inurl: searches for the specific string in the url. It is useful when we are looking for specific pages like login page.

   For example: inurl:"login.php"

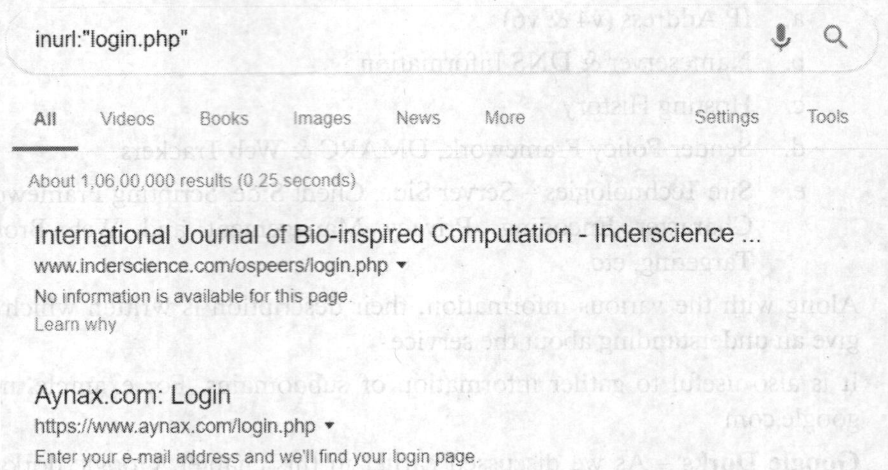

c. **intitle:** it will filter the pages and show the only results having specified string in HTML Title of the page.

   For example: intitle:"Cyber Square"

d. **filetype:** it searches for the specific file type. Sometimes we are looking for the pdf or ppt files but we get many irrelevant results, this dork is useful in such cases.

   For example: filetype:pdf "hacking"

These are some of the basic google dorks with their usage example. There is a long list of google dorks and you can refer to the following resources for practising more dorks.

https://gist.github.com/stevenswafford/393c6ec7b5375d5e8cdc
https://nfsec.pl/media/ghdb.pdf
https://gbhackers.com/latest-google-dorks-list/

3. **Whois Information** – According to ICANN, the term "WHOIS" refers to protocols, services, and data types associated with Internet naming and numbering resources beyond domain names, such as Internet Protocol (IP) addresses, and Autonomous System Numbers (ASNs). The WHOIS service includes WHOIS clients, WHOIS servers, WHOIS data stores, and WHOIS data (domain name registration records). Essentially, WHOIS can refer to any of the following:

   a. The information that is collected at the time of registration of a domain name or IP numbering resource and subsequently made available via the WHOIS Service, and potentially updated throughout the life of the resource.
   b. The WHOIS Protocol itself, which is defined in RFC 3912.
   c. The WHOIS Services that provide public access to domain name registration information typically via applications that implement the WHOIS protocol or a web-based interface.

   The above-mentioned information about WHOIS is as described in the documentation provided by the ICANN.

   In simple term, Whois is a simple tool which can be used to determine who's there sitting behind the domain name and what are various objects like IP Address, Name Server, Server Information, etc. associated with it. Whois provides a very useful set of information and you will find Whois under information gathering or footprinting methods everywhere.

Gathering Whois Information

a. Visit https://whois.icann.org/en
b. Enter the domain name and click on **Lookup.**

www.cybersquareinfo.com | Lookup

c. Confirm your Human Identity by verifying Captcha.
d. It will display the following information –
   a. Contact Information for Admin, Domain Registrant and Tech.
   b. Registrar Company & Status
   c. Domain Expiration Dates (it is useful because sometimes owner forget to re-purchase the domain and once it's expired, you can purchase the same domain)
   d. Name Server Information
   e. Raw Whois Records which contains the same above information.

There are various other website(s) to find whois information, some are:
http://whois.domaintools.com/
https://whois.net/
https://in.godaddy.com/whois
https://www.enom.com/whois/
In further chapter(s), we will also look at accessing whois information using command line.

4. **Viewing Web Archives** – Way Back Machine (archive.org) is a powerful web interface project which is a digital library of internet archives and is actively working since 1996. It has a huge database of web pages, audio recording, text and much more.

   According to archive.org, The Internet Archive, a 501(c)(3) non-profit, is building a digital library of Internet sites and other cultural artefacts in digital form. Like a paper library, it provides free access to researchers, historians, scholars, the print disabled, and the general public. Our mission is to provide Universal Access to All Knowledge.

   It began in 1996 by archiving the Internet itself, a medium that was just beginning to grow in use. Like newspapers, the content published on the web was ephemeral - but unlike newspapers, no one was saving it. Today it has 20+ years of web history accessible through the Wayback Machine and it work with 450+ library and other partners through its Archive-It program to identify important web pages. Today its archive contains:

   - 330 billion web pages
   - 20 million books and texts
   - 4.5 million audio recordings (including 180,000 live concerts)
   - 4 million videos (including 1.6 million Television News programs)
   - 3 million images
   - 200,000 software programs

   The above-mentioned statistics and information are as provided by the archive.org, for more information you can read it there.

Using Way Back Machine

a. Visit https://archive.org/
b. Enter website address and press enter.

c. It will show a year and a calendar timeline. Select a year on year timeline to open calendar timeline for the particular year. (refer to the screenshot below)

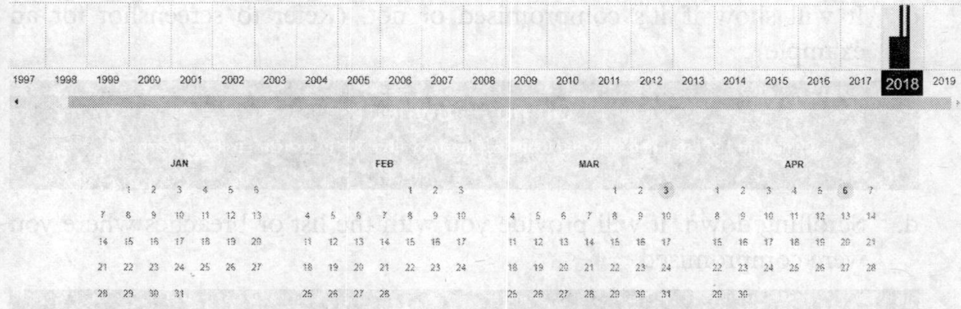

e. The dates having circles contains a snapshot of change *i.e.* whenever a change occurs, it stores the snapshot of the particular day, which shows the before update webpage. Click on any of the circle to check the webpage of that day,

Using Internet Archive

a. Visit https://archive.org/

b. Enter Search Query String & click on the go.

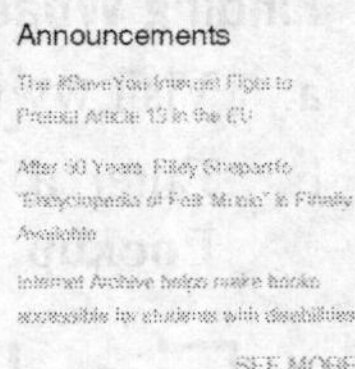

c. It will show the relevant results, we can also change the search type and perform advanced search.

d. There are wide array of digital documents, audio, video and software can be crawled.

There are many other interesting open source projects developed by the same organization, you can find and explore them at - https://archive.org/projects/

5. Have I Been Pwned – haveibeenpwned.com

It is a web application which keeps the records of the data breaches and helps you to check if you have been part of any breach. It asks for the email address and checks for its association with data breaches. (Please note that it only checks for the breaches it stores, there might be some which are untraced) Follow the step to check –

a. Visit https://haveibeenpwned.com/

b. Enter your email address and click on **pwned?**

c. It will show if it's compromised or not. (Refer to screenshot for an example)

Oh no — pwned!

Pwned on 164 breached sites and found 239 pastes (subscribe to search sensitive breaches)

d. Scrolling down, it will provide you with the list of breaches where you were compromised.

Breaches you were pwned in

A "breach" is an incident where data has been unintentionally exposed to the public. Using the 1Password password manager helps you ensure all your passwords are strong and unique such that a breach of one service doesn't put your other services at risk.

6. BuiltWith – www.builtwith.com

BuiltWith is a web application that is used to find out what websites are built with. Apart from this it provides many other services and products such as keywords list, cyber risk auditing, etc.

Finding What Websites are built with using BuiltWith

a. Visit www.builtwith.com

b. Enter a Website, Technology or Keyword for Lookup and click on **Lookup.**

Find out what websites are Built With

cybersquareinfo.com

Lookup

c. It will provide a list of technologies used which includes:

   a. Widgets & Plugins
   b. Frameworks
   c. Mobile Components
   d. Content Delivery Network (CDN)
   e. Javascript & Other Programmable Libraries & APIs
   f. Email & Web Hosting Providers
   g. SSL Certificates
   h. Web Servers & Operating System Information
   i. Syndication Techniques, etc.

Now this retrieves us a very useful piece of information because knowing what programming languages have been used or finding the operating system

& server platforms we can look for platform specific vulnerabilities to hack into our target system. Sometimes, it becomes very complex to start a pentest without knowing anything about the target system. Such tools help in these cases.

7. **Wappalyzer** – Wappalyzer is yet another tool for identifying technologies used on the websites. According to Wappalyzer Documentation, it's a cross-platform utility that uncovers the technologies used on websites. It detects content management systems, e-commerce platforms, web frameworks, server software, analytics tools and many more.

It comes as a browser extension and available for popular browsers like Google Chrome and Mozilla Firefox. It can also be used from its web application. It also provides a list of Market Leaders in respective technology domains.

Technology Lookup Using Wappalyzer

Method – 1: Using Web Application

a. Visit https://www.wappalyzer.com/
b. Scroll to Technology Lookup Section, provide target URL & Click on Search icon and it will show results as shown below:

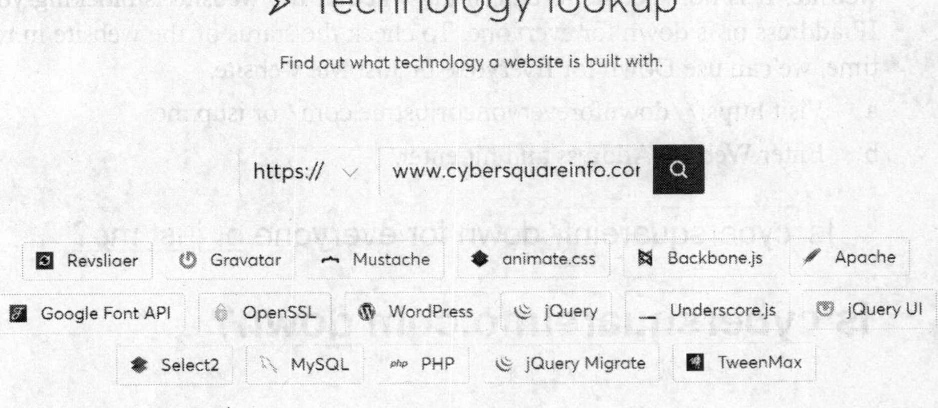

Method – 2: Using Browser Extension

a. Visit https://www.wappalyzer.com/download
b. Download Extension for your respective browser and activate it.

Browser extensions

Install Wappalyzer in your browser to see the technologies used on websites you visit at a glance.

c. Restart your browser & Wappalyzer Extension will be visible in extension toolbar.

d. Visit the target website and click on Wappalyzer Icon and it will show a popup with major technologies used.

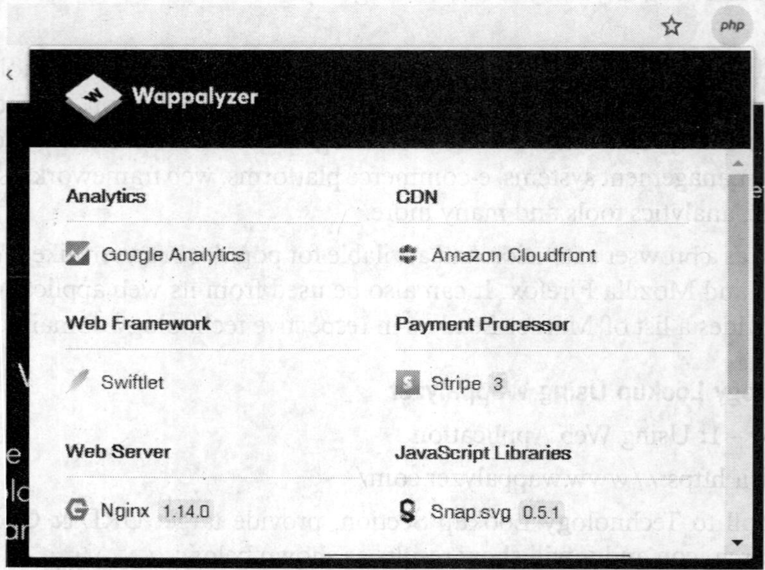

8. **Website Downtime Status** – Sometimes, we are unable to access a particular website. It is not specific to determine whether the website is blocking your IP address or is down for everyone. To check the status of the website in real time, we can use Down for Everyone or Just Me website.

   a. Visit https://downforeveryoneorjustme.com/ or isup.me

   b. Enter Website Address and hit enter.

Is cybersquareinf(down for everyone or just me?

Is cybersquareinfo.com down?

It's just you. cybersquareinfo.com is up.

A. It provides other services just as malware scanning, looking for website owners, etc.

9. **CentralOps** – www.centralops.net

CentralOps.net is a web application which contains many free online network and domain tools such as domain & email dossier, ping, traceroute, nslookup, etc.

We will perform few tools among many present at CenntralOps.

Visit www.centralops.net

Domain Dossier – It Investigate domains and IP addresses. Get registrant information, DNS records, and more—all in one report.

a. Enter Domain or IP Address & click on Go.

enter a domain or IP address

cybersquareinfo.com go

or learn about yourself

b. It will result in the following information –

   a. IP Address Lookup
   b. Domain Whois Record
   c. Network Whois Record
   d. DNS Record
   e. Service Scan & Traceroute (if selected)

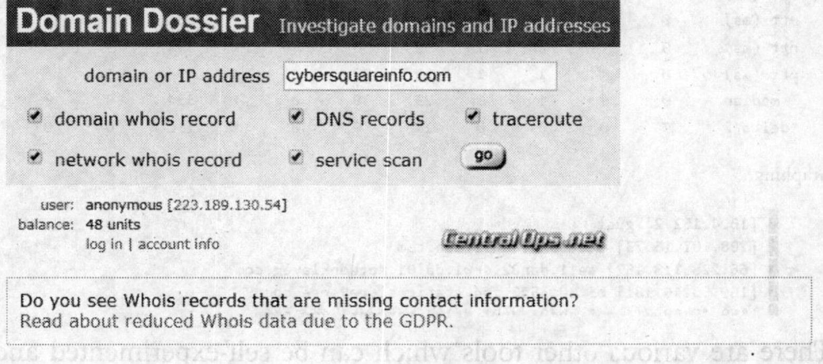

Address lookup

canonical name **cybersquareinfo.com.**

aliases

addresses **23.94.69.34**

Domain Whois record

Queried **whois.internic.net** with **"dom cybersquareinfo.com"**...

Browser Mirror – It tells what browser reveals information about the user.

a. Click on Browser Mirror.

b. Under **Cookies** Sections, Click on Complete Test.

c. It will result with following information –

   a. Client IP Address & Server Port
   b. Request & Encryption Type
   c. Http Headers
   d. Cookies
   e. Client-Side Scripting Information, etc.

Analyse Path – It is an experimental Graphical Traceroute service. Traceroute is used to count no. of hops (routers) between two hosts.

a. Click on Analyze Path and provide target ip address in **to field** & click on **Go.** You can also set data points manually.

b. The output will look like the image below –

from **hexillion.com [208.101.16.74]**

to 223.189.130.54

data points 5 (higher = more accurate)

Go

Collecting data on path to **223.189.130.54 [223.189.130.54]**...

hop	1	2	3	4	5	6	7	8	9	10	11	12	13
rtt (ms)	0	*	1	1	29	30	*	*	334	*	*	*	*
rtt (ms)	0	*	1	1	29	30	*	*	334	*	*	*	*
rtt (ms)	0	*	1	1	29	30	*	*	334	*	*	*	*
rtt (ms)	0	*	3	1	32	30	*	*	334	*	*	*	*
rtt (ms)	0	*	1	1	29	30	*	*	334	*	*	*	*
median	0	0	1	1	29	30	0	0	334	0	0	0	0
delta/2	0	0	0	0	14	0	0	0	152	0	0	0	0

Graphing...

```
[10.4.152.2] gust
[208.101.16.73] outbound.hexillion.com
[66.228.118.157] ae11.dar02.sr01.dal01.networklayer.com
[169.53.16.181] b5.10.35a9.ip4.static.sl-reverse.com
```

There are various other tools which can be self-experimented and are easy to use. Throughout, we will encounter at many web applications having almost, same tools, but their output may differ and give some additional set of information.

10. MX Tool Box – www.mxtoolbox.com

It is yet another website which provides many tools and services for free (paid services are also present), like –

a. Mx Lookup
b. DNS Lookup for IP Address
c. Smtp test
d. DNS Server Check
e. IP Security Key Lookup
f. Domain Health Report
g. Website Query
h. ICMP Echo Request
i. Subnet Calculator
j. DNS Propagation Check

k. DMARC Report Analyzer
l. Password Generator
m. ASN Lookup
n. DNS Lookup for location

And many others. (www.mxtoolbox.com/NetworkTools.aspx)

We will look at a demonstration of some tools and other tools can be explored by the user in the same fashion.

Visit www.mxtoolbox.com/NetworkTools.aspx

(Keep All Tools Tabs Open)

MX Lookup

MX Lookup is used for **Mail Server** Information Lookup. It searches for mail server related entries in DNS Records and returns the specific information.

a. Enter the target URL in **MX Box** and click on the Play button. It will redirect to a new page with the result.

b. Results will give information like Mail Service Provider, etc. (Refer to image below) –

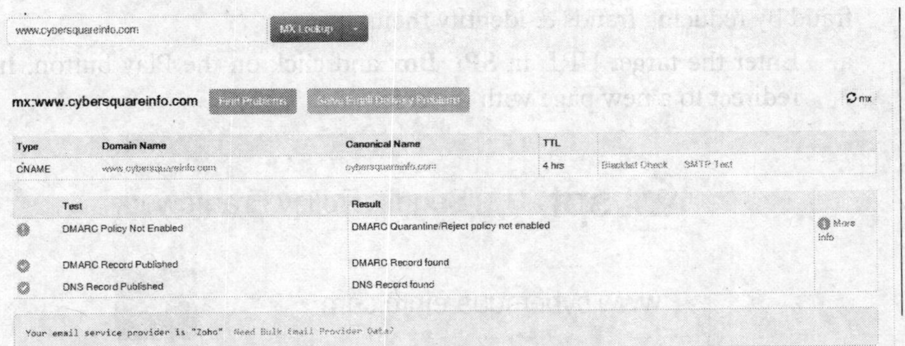

SMTP Test

SMTP refers to Simple Mail Transfer Protocol and operates on **Port 25.** This tool queries this protocol to analyse for various tests like Banner Check, Reverse DNS Match, Valid Hostname, Open Replay, etc.

c. Enter the target URL in **SMTP Box** and click on the Play button. It will redirect to a new page with the result.

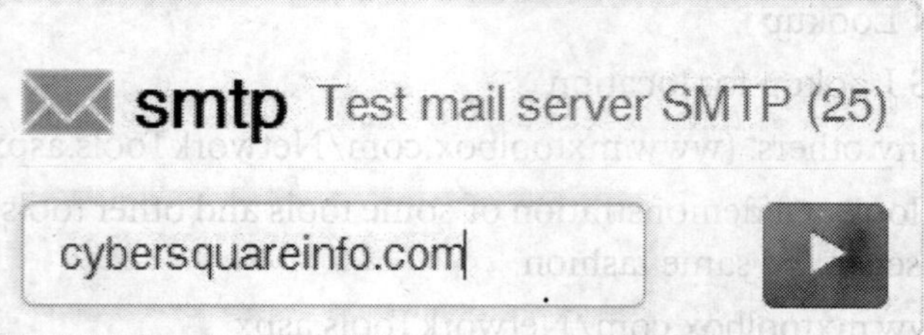

d. Results will look like the image below –

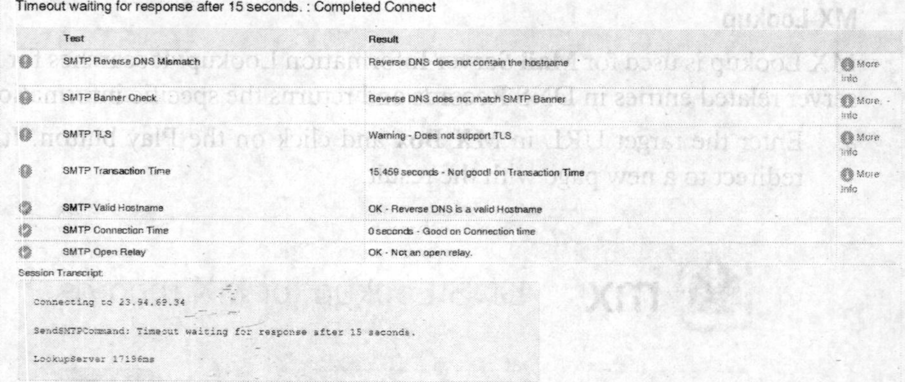
Timeout waiting for response after 15 seconds. : Completed Connect

	Test	Result	
	SMTP Reverse DNS Mismatch	Reverse DNS does not contain the hostname	More info
	SMTP Banner Check	Reverse DNS does not match SMTP Banner	More info
	SMTP TLS	Warning - Does not support TLS	More info
	SMTP Transaction Time	15.459 seconds - Not good! on Transaction Time	More info
	SMTP Valid Hostname	OK - Reverse DNS is a valid Hostname	
	SMTP Connection Time	0 seconds - Good on Connection time	
	SMTP Open Relay	OK - Not an open relay.	

Session Transcript

```
Connecting to 23.94.69.34

SendSMTPCommand: Timeout waiting for response after 15 seconds.

LookupServer 17196ms
```

SPF Lookup

SPF (Sender's Policy Framework) is a type of record which allows domain owners to publish a list of IP Address or Subnets that are authorized to send emails on their behalf. It works towards minimizing the amount of spam & fraud by reducing frauds & identity thefts.

a. Enter the target URL in **SPF Box** and click on the Play button. It will redirect to a new page with the result.

b. The results will contain information related to sender policies implemented on the target website.

Domain Health Report

The Domain Health Check will execute hundreds of domain/email/network performance tests to make sure all of your systems are online and performing optimally. The report will then return results for your domain and highlight critical problem areas for your domain that need to be resolved.

c. Enter the target URL in **Domain Box** and click on the Play button. It will redirect to a new page with the result.

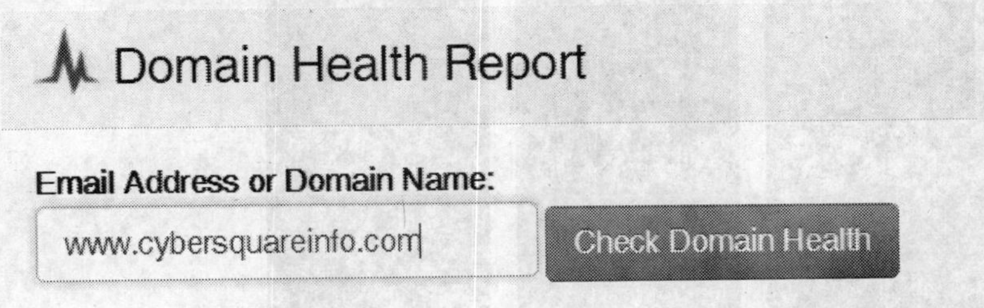

d. The result provides information in four major categories
   i. Problems – Errors, Warnings & Checks Passed
   ii. Blacklist - Errors, Warnings & Checks Passed
   iii. Mail Server - Errors, Warnings & Checks Passed
   iv. Web Server - Errors, Warnings & Checks Passed
   v. DNS - Errors, Warnings & Checks Passed

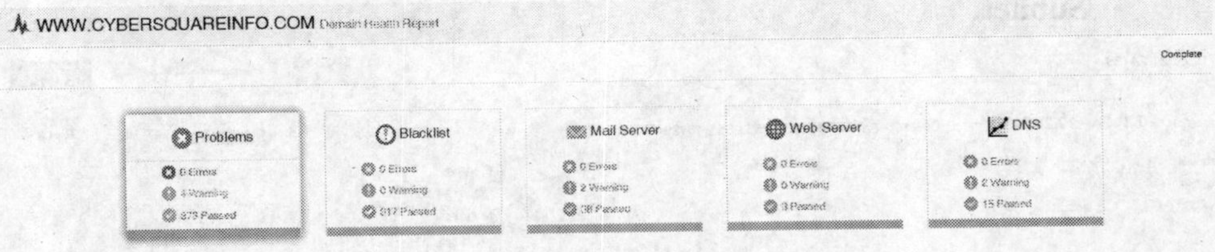

Password Generator

This password generator tool will generate 15 secure, random passwords which are designed to meet the requirements of most systems. It also generates passwords in several categories for your convenience, including one that should be easy to pronounce and remember.

a. Click on **Password Generator.**

b. It will show a list of randomly generated passwords with three categories–
   i. Easy to Remember
   ii. Stronger
   iii. Very Strong

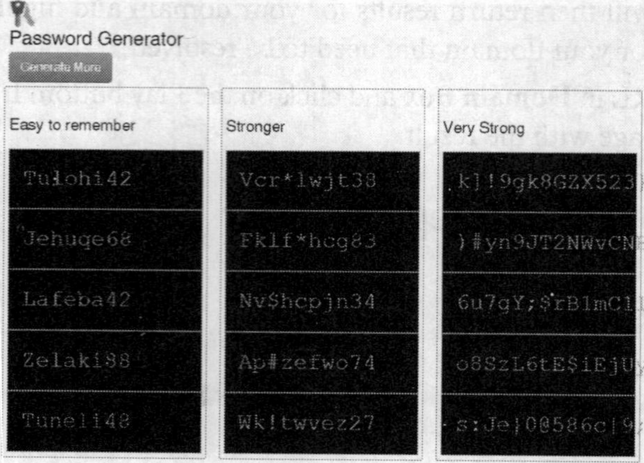

Subnet Calculator

The subnet calculator lets you enter a subnet range (CIDR) and see IP address information about that range. It also lists each IP address in the range and automatically does a Reverse IP Lookup for you.

a. Click on **Subnet Calculator.**

b. Provide IP Address or Subnet & Optional Mask and click on **View Subnet.**

c. If you want to monitor the specific IP, you need to register and have an account.

There are variety of tools which are handy and easy to explore. You can see the basic information about the tool just by clicking on it.

There are many other websites which provide such tools, some important websites are –

1. https://network-tools.com/
2. https://tools.dnsstuff.com

Summary

This chapter summarizes various basic methods and online tools which can be used to gather intel about various services. We have looked for a wide array of services. In the Next chapter we will look at use of Open Source Tools for Information Gathering.

7 Open Source Information Gathering

Module Outlines

- Introduction to OSINT
- Gray Literature
- Advantages of Open Source Information Gathering
- Open Source Intelligence Methods

Open Source technologies, resources and tools are widely used & is getting great popularity among the whole IT Sector. Open Source allows distribution of tools, technologies and resources under a various open license and allows anyone to use, contribute, modify and reproduce it. It allows the developers to contribute and produce great software & everything happens for free.

Linux is one of the biggest open source projects. There are many popular open source projects available in the market which we use in day to day technology work as well. Git, the technology we discussed in PART – 1 is again an open source project and GitHub, built around git, is one of the biggest platforms for managing open source tools and resources.

In this chapter, we will look at various resources for gathering information and scrapping intel using various Open Source Platforms. Let's first look at what Open Source can get us –

a. Social Media & Other User Names
b. Email Address associated with various websites
c. Domain Name & IP Address related Information
d. Multimedia, Webcam, Tools, Documents & Other Information.
e. People Search Engines
f. Business and Public Archives
g. Classified Information
h. Dark Web and Terrorism Information
i. Exploits & other vulnerability related information
j. Threat & Cyber Intelligence

k. Data Leaks and associated websites

l. Government Record Intel

m. Technical Information such as Link Extractions, Website Mirroring, IT Device Default Credentials, Web Statistics and Analysis, etc.

The scope of open source information gathering and intelligence is not limited to the above mentioned parameter. It can get us almost everything and a specific piece of information we are looking for. Further, in this chapter, we will look at various open source methodologies for Intel Generation. Before that, we will look at various important aspects to get a deep understanding of the open source.

Gray Literature – Gray literature is the general name for non-formally published scholarly or substantive information (often found on the internet and in specialized resources; often not formally peer-reviewed; especially important in all kinds of sciences) such as:

- theses and dissertations
- technical reports
- working papers
- evaluation reports
- conference proceedings
- publications from NGOs, INGOs, think tanks and policy institutes
- patents
- preprints

(The above-mentioned information about Gray Literature is as provided by http://guides.library.cornell.edu/graylit. You can get more information about gray literature on the same website.)

Organizations or Individuals interested in Open Source Information are:

1. Government
2. Law Enforcement Agencies
3. Intelligence Agencies
4. Privacy – cautious individuals
5. Business Owners
6. Penetration Testers & Black Hat Hackers
7. Terrorist Organizations

Advantages of Open Source Information Gathering:

1. Cost Effective – Open source information is free to use (in most scenarios) which makes it less expensive compared to other methods of information collection and generation.
2. Easy to Access – With proper skills to analyse and use intelligence derived from Open Source Platforms, it becomes very handy and useful to work with OSINT.

3. Reduce In-Person Spying Cost – It highly reduces the cost of spying through a person in the context of both life and money. Especially, it is specific to intelligence agency work.
4. Reduced Legal & Other Authority Issues – Since open source platforms allow the use and reproduction of provided information, it is less likely to lend into legal issues.

Further, in this chapter, we will look at various methods for utilizing open source information. Some of the techniques of information gathering that we have used in the previous chapter(s) may also be used in this section as well. We will look at various services and their alternatives as well.

Open Source Intelligence

1. User Name, Email Address & Profile Crawling

It is easier to find user name, email address and other personal profiling of a person or organizational body using public information. We authorize our social media and email account with different applications & data leakage of that application may reveal the sensitive information to public databases of breached information.

a. Stalkscan.com – StalkScan is a tool that shows all public information for a given Facebook profile. It doesn't involve any hack or hacking; it just displays public info from Facebook's official graph search.

Using this website which generates the results on the basis of Facebook's own graph search which a powerful search engine that let you play with the big data collected & mined by Facebook.

a. Enter the **target profile url** & hit enter (or click on search glass icon). It will show a Profile with numeric id loaded.

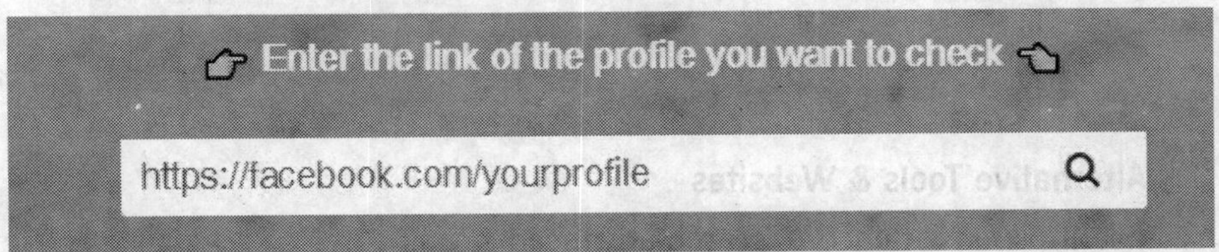

b. Below, it will show various options to look for like Profile, Tags, Comments, People & Places.

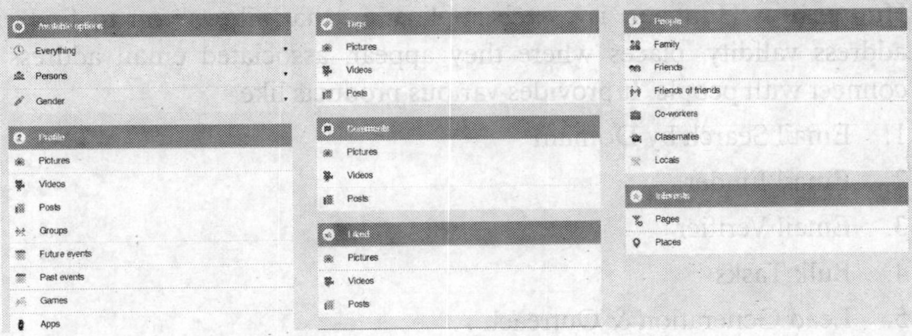

c. Click on desired button to look for information & it will open a new tab with Facebook query.

https://www.facebook.com/search/100002201231837/relatives/intersect

Harsh Bothra's relatives

Alternative Websites

a. http://graph.tips/beta/
b. https://peoplefindthor.dk/
c. http://netbootcamp.org/facebook.html

b. Followerwonk.com – It is a web-based twitter analytic tool which allows various features for analysis including Follower Tracking, Bio Search, Compare Users & Analyze, etc.

a. Visit www.followerwonk.com & choose any one tab among various options like Search Bios or Compare Users.
b. Provide Keyword, it may be random word, username or category and choose between search twitter profiles or search twitter bios only
c. It will show results which will include details like **no. of tweets, following, followers, account age & social authority.**

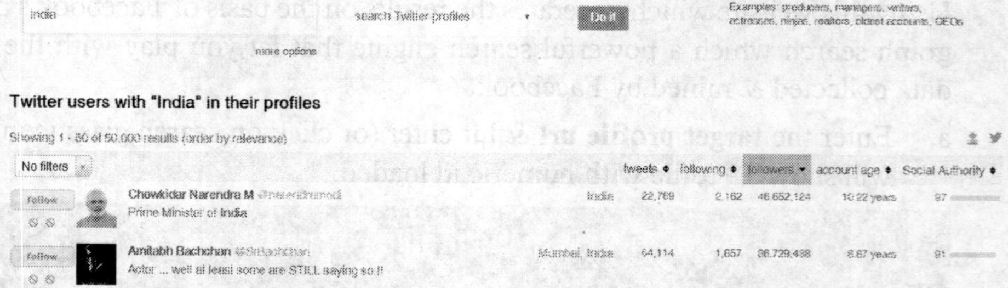

Alternative Tools & Websites

a. https://twitter.com/search-advanced
b. https://www.exporttweet.com/
c. http://sleepingtime.org/

c. Hunter.io – Hunter.io is a web application that allows you to find email address validity, places where they appear, associated email address and connect with people. It provides various products like

1. Email Search by Domain
2. Email Finder
3. Email Verifier
4. Bulk Tasks
5. Lead Generation & Outreach

We will look at Email Search by Domain, follow the steps below:

a. Visit https://hunter.io/search
b. Enter Target Domain in Domain Search Box & Hit Enter.
c. You can apply filters for specific search, export results into CSV, save the lead and check the source of email finding (if available).

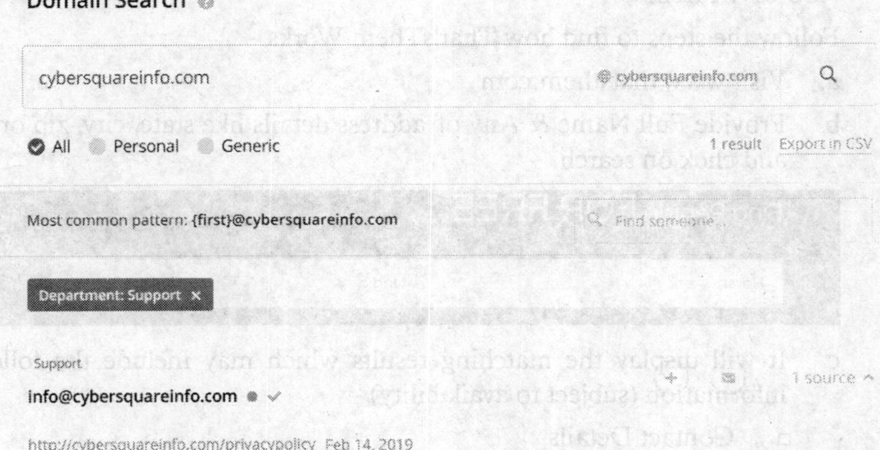

This is a very interesting tools to find out associated emails with domain name. in many cases, we are not able to find valid email addresses of an organization by simple lookup or by crawling their web application. This tool makes the whole task easy & results in useful finding.

There are also video tutorials available for each product.

Alternative Tools & Websites

a. https://www.peoplelooker.com/email-lookup/
b. https://domainbigdata.com/
c. https://tools.verifyemailaddress.io/

d. Data Breach Record Search – These search tools keep an updated record of data breaches and compromised account in them. It can be used to check if a person has been compromised or an email, account or password is leaked online.

We have already looked a similar web-based tool **haveibeenpwned** in the previous chapter(s). There are some of the **Alternate Tools & Websites** –

a. https://dehashed.com/
b. https://intelx.io/
c. https://search.weleakinfo.com/
d. https://leakedsource.ru/

e. People Search – People Search Engine allows to find information about a person which may include details like phone no, address, age, interest, wealth

& other sensitive information. Hackers use such type of information to find their potential targets for social engineering based cyber frauds or some other form of frauds. For intelligence purpose, it can be a handy tool to figure out information about a person involved in a crime. There are many websites available for this, we will look at **thatsthem.com** That's Them Web application allows People Search, Phone Search, Reverse Email Lookup, IP Search & Address Search.

Follow the steps to find how That'sThem Works –

a. Visit www.thatsthem.com
b. Provide Full Name & Any of address details like state, city, zip or street and click on search.

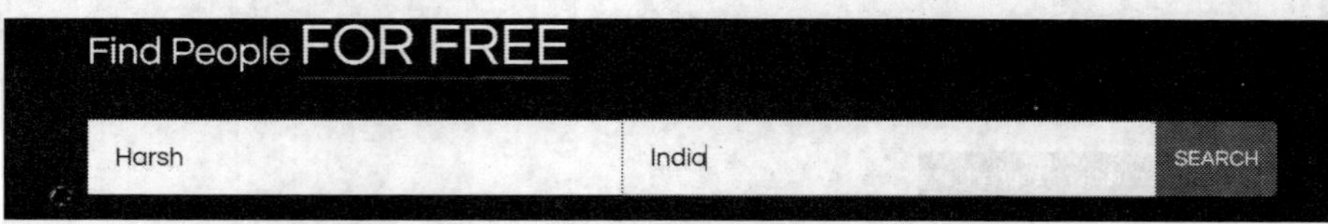

c. It will display the matching results which may include the following information (subject to availability) –
   - Contact Details
   - IP Address
   - Wealth, Tech, Shopping, Travel & Other Scores
   - Estimated Net Worth & Income
   - Education, Occupation & Language
   - Age Group.

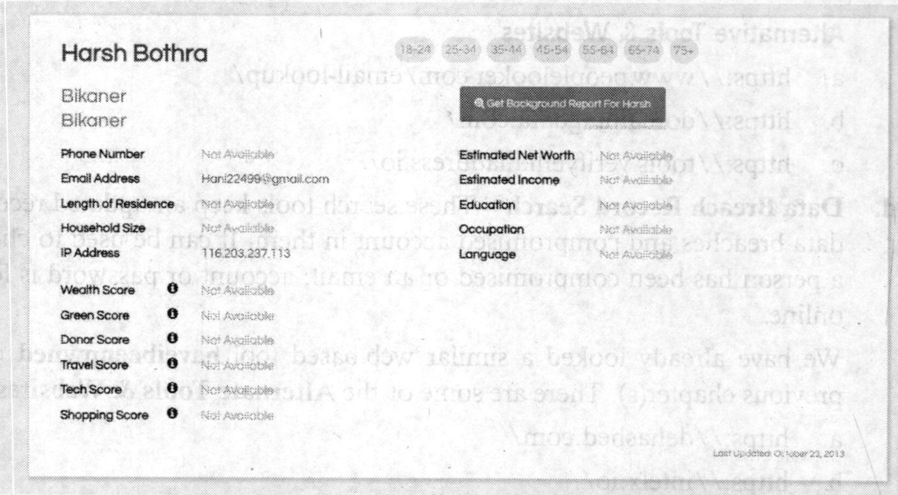

Alternate Tools & Websites

a. https://pipl.com/
b. **http://ufind.name/**

c. https://publicrecords.directory/

d. https://www.spytox.com/

e. https://inteltechniques.com/menu/pages/person.tool.html

2. IT Device Default Credentials

According to various surveys, reports & archives, many of the IT Devices such as Routers, IoT Devices, Network enabled smart devices, etc. are prone to be compromised because they use default credentials.

Default credentials are pre-configured for initial authentication to the devices and are required to be changed after that. However, most of the people, either due to lack of awareness or due to ease of remembering (or some other reasons), don't change the default credentials & are compromised easily. There are various sources which provide default credentials which are usually filtered by **Company Name, Device Type, Device/Model Id or another distinguisher.** You can visit these websites, look for your target device and try default credentials for authentication.

Some of the websites to find default credentials are:

a. https://cirt.net/passwords

b. http://routerpasswords.com/

c. http://open-sez.me/

d. https://hashes.org/

e. http://phenoelit.org/dpl/dpl.html

3. Vulnerabilities Databases

According to various surveys, there are a huge number of services, operating systems, networks, devices, web applications and other computational targets which are prone to being compromised by the existing and already discovered vulnerabilities because of various reasons including not patching service for a long time, ignoring updates, developer or architect design flow issues, etc.

There are various vulnerability databases which store records of various vulnerability, patch and exploit information, etc. These records can be used to exploit target devices or services.

Some of the websites & databases to look for Vulnerabilities are –

a. https://www.exploit-db.com/

b. https://nvd.nist.gov/

c. https://0day.today/

d. https://www.owasp.org/

e. https://packetstormsecurity.com/

4. Webcams Search & Lookup

Over the internet, there are tons of webcams & **web-based multimedia & image** processing devices which are vulnerable and exposed. Anyone can access the exposed webcams and it is sometimes useful when you find the webcam of location you are willing to spy or sneak-peek, exposed and open to access.

Some of the websites to look exposed & open webcams are –

a. http://world-webcams.nsspot.net/
b. https://www.livefromiceland.is/
c. http://www.insecam.org/

5. *Search Engines*

Search Engine is one of the most important tools in daily life, and as a general practice, most of the users interact with search engines such as Google, Yahoo or Bing. Search Engines indexes and lists mappings of various queries to similar and relevant web pages & resources. There are various search engines apart from most commonly used ones like Google. These search engines can be used to perform specific searches, privacy-oriented searches, etc.

A. General Search Engines

a. Google
b. Bing
c. Yahoo
d. Ask
e. AOL
f. Millionshort
g. Factbites
h. GoodSearch, etc.

B. Popular National Search Engines

a. Yandex (Russia)
b. Baidu (China)
c. Daum (South Korea)
d. Goo (Japan), Etc.

C. Privacy Oriented Search Engines

e. DuckDuckGo
f. Gigablast
g. Gibiru
h. Peekier
i. StartPage, Etc.

D. IoT Devices Search Engines

a. ZoomEye
b. Lookr
c. EarthCam
d. Censys
e. Thingful
f. Thingverse
g. Pictimo
h. Reolink, Etc.

E. Other Search Engines

a. Global File Search (FTP Based)
b. File Watcher (FTP Based)
c. Search (Metadata Based)
d. Zapmeta (Metadata Based)
e. Google Images
f. Imgur
g. Photobucket
h. Flickr
i. Stalkture
j. Websta
k. Pinterest
l. News Press
m. GettyImages
n. Tiny Eye
o. Imagebrief, Etc.

6. Fake News Detection

With advancement and connectivity over social media and internet, people use these sources to spread rumours, fake news, hoaxes and articles that might not fall into public interest and can cause damage to the reputation of the person, society, state or nation. There are some web-based tools or web applications available which may help to identify fake news and rumours to some extent, these websites are:

a. https://www.snopes.com/
b. https://www.factcheck.org/fake-news
c. http://verificationjunkie.com/
d. https://www.truthorfiction.com/
e. https://www.hoax-slayer.com/

7. *Commercial Satellites & Global Date/Time*

Commercial Satellites, Movement of sun and moon during a specified time of the day, weather & geographic details of a place can be analysed using various available platforms online.

a. Wolfram Alpha – a computational intelligence platform, can be used to compute expert-level answers using Wolfram's breakthrough algorithms, knowledgebase and AI technology.

   a. Visit https://www.wolframalpha.com

   b. Enter Keyword you want to know about and it will revert with relevant results based on AI Search.

b. SunCalc – www.suncalc.org

It can be used to track the position of sun during the given time frame of a day.

c. **MoonCalc** – www.mooncalc.org

It can be used to track the position of moon during the given time frame of a day.

8. *Global Terrorism Database*

According to GTD, The Global Terrorism Database (GTD) is an open-source database including information on terrorist events around the world from 1970 through 2017 (with annual updates planned for the future). Unlike many other event databases, the GTD includes systematic data on domestic as well as international terrorist incidents that have occurred during this time period and now includes more than 180,000 cases.

Scope of Data

The GTD was designed to gather a wide variety of etiological and situational variables pertaining to each terrorist incident. Depending on availability of information, the database records up to 120 separate attributes of each incident, including approximately 75 coded variables that can be used for statistical analysis. These are collected under eight broad categories, as identified in the GTD Codebook, and include, whenever possible:

- Incident date
- Region
- Country
- State/province
- City
- Latitude and longitude (beta)
- Perpetrator group name
- Tactic used in attack

- Nature of the target (type and sub-type, up to three targets)
- Identity, corporation, and nationality of the target (up to three nationalities)
- Type of weapons used (type and sub-type, up to three weapons types)
- Whether the incident was considered a success
- If and how a claim(s) of responsibility was made
- Amount of damage, and more narrowly, the amount of united states damage
- Total number of fatalities (persons, united states nationals, terrorists)
- Total number of injured (persons, united states nationals, terrorists)
- Indication of whether the attack is international or domestic
- Other variables provide information unique to specific types of cases, including kidnappings, hostage incidents, and hijackings.

Source - *https://www.start.umd.edu/gtd/using-gtd*

To explore and crawl information using GTD, perform following steps –

a. Visit https://www.start.umd.edu/gtd/

b. Click on New User & it will redirect to a tutorial and explanation section where you can see the details about using GTD.

Searching GTD

Users have three different ways to search for GTD incidents using the website: browsing, keyword search, and the advanced search wizard.

- **Browsing GTD:** Browsing is the least flexible search approach, through which users are given the option to generate a list of all GTD incidents (1970-2017) that share one characteristic, selected by the user.
  - To Browse, using the computer's mouse, select one variable from the list of 6 "Browse by" variables (region, country, perpetrator, weapon type, attack type, or target type).
  - Then, click on the "Go" button.
  - At the next screen, select one value for that variable from the list provided. (For instance, a user can select the value "Chemical" under the variable "Weapon Type".) Once you have clicked on the selected variable value, you'll be taken to the Search Results page, providing information on all GTD cases that reflect the specified characteristics.
- **Search by Keywords:** Users can search all of the text associated with descriptions of GTD incidents by using the keyword Search function. This feature will identify those cases in which the keyword appears in the description of any of the variables for each incident.
  - To Search by Keyword, enter the search term(s) in the Search box, and click on the "Search" button. Once you have clicked on Search,

you'll be taken to the Search Results page, with a list of all GTD incidents that include those term(s) anywhere within the incident's description.

- If a user enters multiple words in the Search box, the Search Results list will include those incidents that include all of the words entered by the user.
- Do not use quotation marks or apostrophes when entering text in this search field.

- **Advanced Search:** This search wizard provides users with the opportunity to identify a collection of search parameters and to conduct a customizes search for the incidents that meet those parameters.

Source – *GTD Website.*

a. In Search Section, type any keyword such as nuclear and click on search

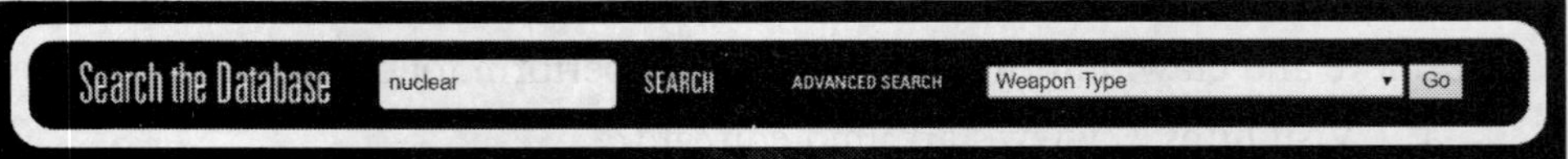

b. It will show various options for chart visualization of results found. Scroll down to see the list of results and click on any GTD id to see its report.

c. A report will look like below image & this might help in some investigations where a link is found with some terrorist attacks or organizations.

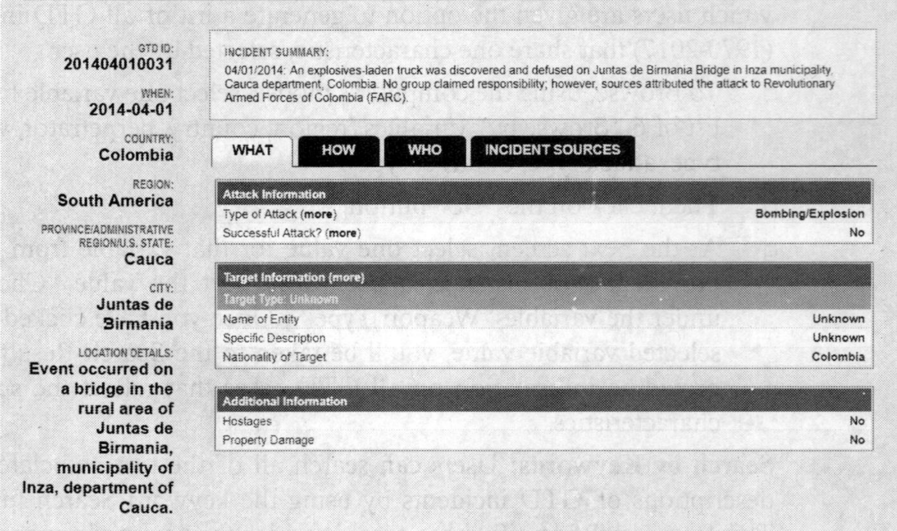

9. *OpSec – Operational Security*

OPSEC is can consider to be originated as a military term which provides and underlines various strategies, measures and controls to prevent potential adversaries from discovering critical operations-related data. Since, the use of digital information and strategic planning is growing in every sector, OpSec is now one of the important aspects of Businesses as well.

OpSec Process

a. **Identification of Critical Information** which may include sensitive, harmful or confidential information which needs to be protected or restricted from external or internet use/leakage.

b. **Threat Modelling** procedure involves determining threats to the organization's infrastructure, reputation, critical or sensitive information, which may lead to severe impact on the organization, if mishandled.

c. **Vulnerability & Risk Assessment** is important phase where potential weakness, bugs and security issues are identified and risk associate with each of them is properly analysed.

d. **Countermeasures** are applied by the Risk & Threat Level and the severity of the vulnerability as a final approach to ensure information integrity and security improvements.

10. Persona Creation

Persona creation methods and techniques allows to generating a fake identity or persona which can be used for various purposes including intelligence. This technique is generally adopted by attackers to hide behind a fake identity to perform attacks. It is highly recommended to use it for legal purposes only or with having authority.

a. **Faker.js** – It is based on node.js (a javascript framework) for generating fake identities.

   a. Visit https://cdn.rawgit.com/Marak/faker.js/master/examples/browser/index.html
   b. Choose Locality and Click on Generate New.
   c. It will generate Random Data including Name, Birth, Address, Phone, Username, Password, Email & Avatar.

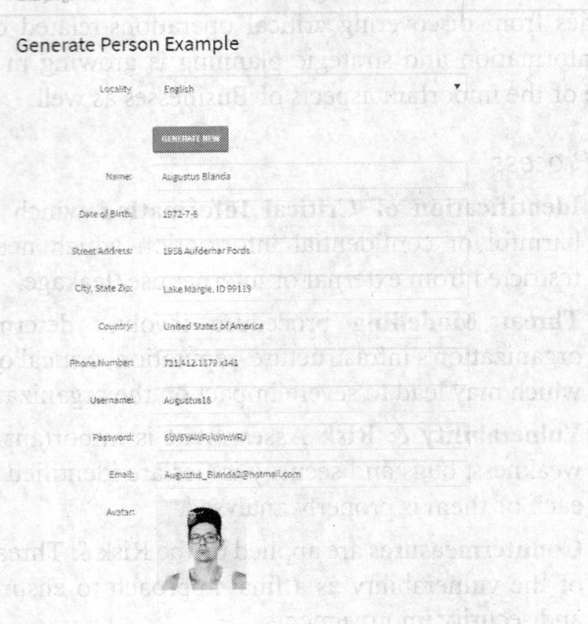

Alternative Websites

a. https://www.fakenamegenerator.com/
b. https://backgroundchecks.org/justdeleteme/fake-identity-generator/
c. https://randomuser.me/

11. The Invisible Internet Project (I2P)

According to I2P, I2P is an anonymous network, exposing a simple layer that applications can use to anonymously and securely send messages to each other. The network itself is strictly message based (a la IP), but there is a library available to allow reliable streaming communication on top of it (a la TCP). All communication is end to end encrypted (in total there are four layers of encryption used when sending a message), and even the end points ("destinations") are cryptographic identifiers (essentially a pair of public keys).

Download & Install I2P by visiting –

https://geti2p.net/en/download

Post-install work

- After running the installer on windows, simply click on the "Start I2P" button which will bring up the router console, which has further instructions.
- On Unix-like systems, I2P can be started as a service using the "i2prouter" script, located in the directory you selected for I2P. Changing to that

directory in a console and issuing "sh i2prouter status" should tell you the router's status. The arguments "start", "stop" and "restart" control the service. The router console can be accessed at its usual location. For users on OpenSolaris and other systems for which the wrapper (i2psvc) is not supported, start the router with "sh runplain.sh" instead.

- When installing for the first time, please remember to adjust your NAT/ firewall if you can, bearing in mind the Internet-facing ports I2P uses, described here among other ports. If you have successfully opened your port to inbound TCP, also enable inbound TCP on the configuration page.
- Also, please review and adjust the bandwidth settings on the configuration page, as the default settings of 96 KBps down / 40 KBps up are fairly slow.
- If you want to reach eepsites via your browser, have a look on the browser proxy setup page for an easy how-to.

Source – I2P Post – Install Work Documentation

Summary

Throughout this chapter, we have a look at various aspects of Open Source Intelligence & Open Source Information Gathering along with its usage. OSINT practices are very important, and it required practice over various tools and methods for better understanding and getting handy. The scope of OSINT is not limited to various tools and methods mentioned in this chapter, and there are various other aspects which can be self-explored.

To learn more about OSINT, Tools, Techniques & Resources, below are the recommended and personally bookmarked resources to follow –

a. www.osintframework.com
b. www.osint.link
c. www.inteltechniques.com

PART-3

ADVANCE TECHNIQUES, SCANNING & ENUMERATION

8 Advanced Information Gathering

Module Outlines

- Introduction to Advanced Information Gathering
- Shodan & working Shodan Products
- Working with Censys
- Working with CyberChef
- Working with FOCA
- Working with Creepy
- Working with Dmitry
- Working with Sublist3r
- Working with Recon-ng
- Working with P0f
- Working with Sparta
- Working with Netdiscover
- Working with Maltego
- Working with TIDoS

The Process of Penetration Testing, Cyber Security Research & Investigations, Forensics Examination, Vulnerability Assessment or similar scope determining fields requires some piece of useful information or intel to start with. Based on that intel, the scope is determined, and the path of execution & methods of exploitation are formulated. Hence, as a result of this, Information Gathering plays a vital role in the whole process and is essential to master.

According to various resources, surveys and experts, you can hack into anything, if you know the vulnerability is and to find that vulnerability you must have appropriate intel.

In this chapter, we will look at Advance Information Gathering methodologies and tools which included with Information Gathering & OSINT (covered in the previous chapter(s)) will help us to master the topic. Once, you have mastered the

Advanced Methodologies of Information Gathering, the whole process becomes easy and specific.

Shodan – Search Engine for Internet Connected Devices

Shodan is yet another search engine specifically designed for the Internet Connected Devices. In Simple terms, Shodan is a search engine that allows you to find and look for various devices connected on the internet such as webcams, servers, smart devices, routers and port & services running on various web applications & systems. According to shodan.io, Shodan is the world's first search engine for Internet-Connected

It is also being described as a search engine of server request/response metadata *i.e.* whenever a service request or respond to something, an appropriate header is attached to it which can be grabbed (banner grabbing, we will discuss it later in this chapter) to know about the various service parameters and information. It was launch in the year 2009 by computer programmer **John Matherly.**

Today, Shodan is one of the most popular tools among security researchers, and it is widely used. It provides APIs (Application Programmable Interface), and that's why many security tools and scripts such as Maltego supports shodan libraries through tool/script's interface.

To operate/use shodan, visit – www.shodan.io & below attachment shows the interface of shodan.

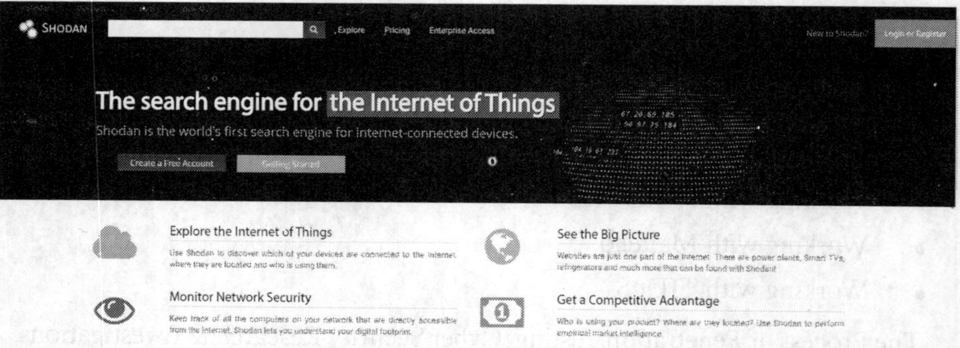

Please Note, to use some of the advanced queries of shodan, it requires to login. It is advised to create a free account for learning purpose before starting to play with Shodan Queries.

Shodan has another product line as well, let's first look into them before starting with Shodan Search Engine. Shodan Products involve tools such as Exploits, Maps, Images, Developer API, Browser Plugins, Shiptracker, Complete guide to shodan, map of the internet, honeypot or not, shodan 3D, etc.

For detailed information, visit - https://www.shodan.io/about/products

Honeyscore – Honeypot or Not

A Honeypot is a technology that is used for computer or network security which helps to detect, counteract or prevent malicious or intentional attempts that may cause a breach or unauthorized access. It is one of the essential mechanisms implemented by Top-Domain Industries.

Honeyscore is a project by Shodan which helps you to identify honeypots. The tool is based on some of the defining properties of honeypots and probability that an IP is a honeypot is captured in a Honeyscore value that can range from 0.0 to 1.0.

Steps to check for Honeypot using Honeyscore –

a. Visit https://honeyscore.shodan.io/
b. Enter suspect IP Address & Click on **Check for Honeypot.**
c. It will tell whether the system is real or is honeypot.
d. The below example shows the IP is a real system.

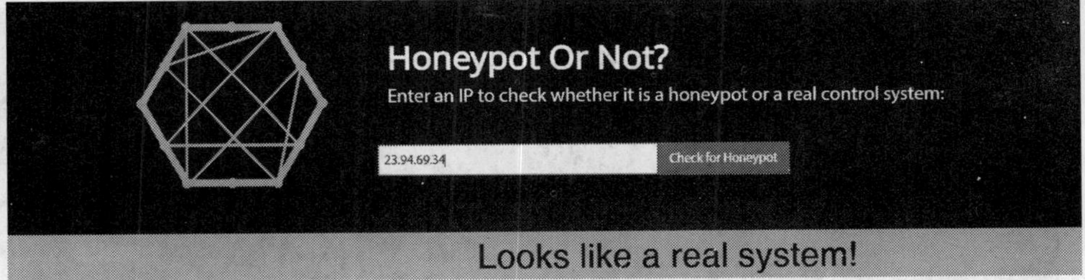

Industrial Control System (ICS) Radar

ICS describes different types of industrial control systems and associated instruments which includes various devices, systems, networks which are used for automating, controlling or managing industrial processes. There are various types of ICS such as **Supervisory Control & Data Acquisition (SCADA) Systems.**

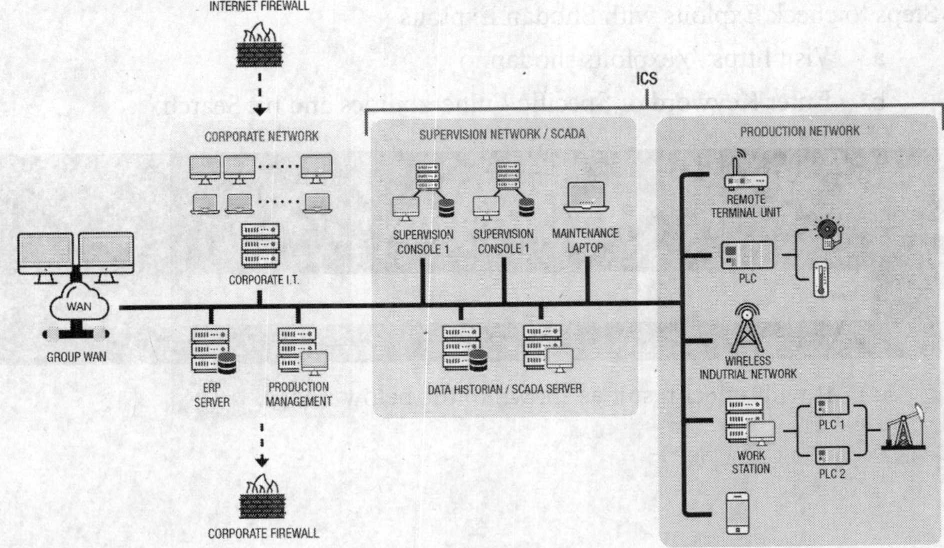

Source - https://www.trendmicro.com/vinfo/us/security/definition/industrial-control-system

Shodan **ICS Radar** crawls the various protocols to fetch raw data and information about ICS. This tool visualizes and shows the location of various ICS Devices & other relevant data.

Steps to view ICS Radar –

a. Visit https://ics-radar.shodan.io/

b. It will show a globe revolving with various green marks hovering which represents various ICS Devices.

c. Below image shows the interface of this tool.

Shodan Exploits

Shodan Exploits is a database or record of exploits stored by shodan. You can type the keyword and search of various exploits. Also, there are few advance queries to search for exploits as well.

Steps to check Exploits with Shodan Exploits –

a. Visit https://exploits.shodan.io

b. Enter Keyword or Specific Vulnerabilities and hit Search.

c. It will reflect result as shown in the below image.

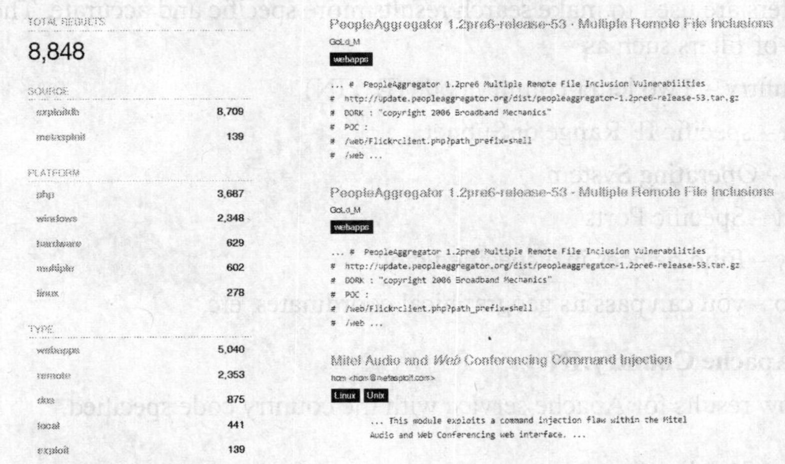

d. Click on any search result to show its report.

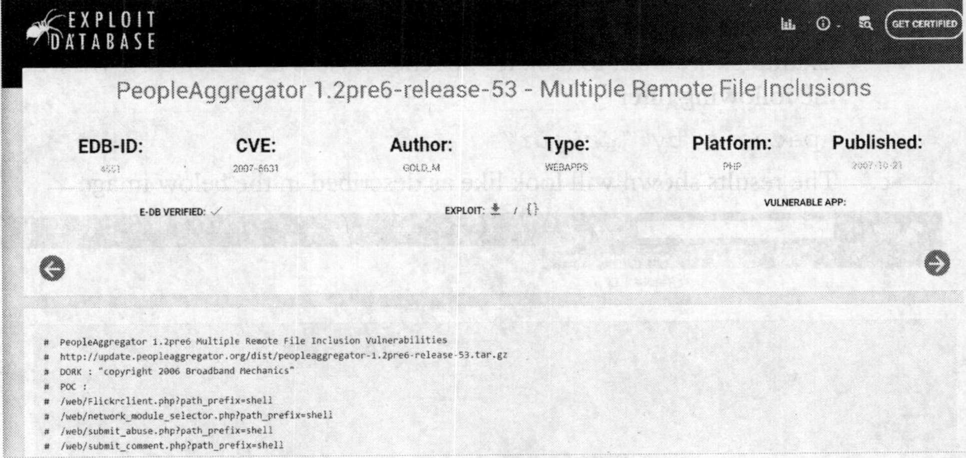

Shodan Search

Shodan Search is the core and heart of shodan.io. It let you find almost everything that is present or connected over the internet from services, open ports & protocols to webcams & IoT Devices.

Shodan is simple to use but take time to master the advanced complex queries. We will look at some of the Shodan search engine queries & further resources to explore Shodan search in depth.

Shodan Basic Operations

Search – Search terms such as keywords, ports, services or anything specific is entered in the search box.

a. Quotation Marks can narrow down the search.

b. Boolean operators such as **+, &, -** can be used to include/exclude query terms and form complex queries.

Filters – Filters are used to make search results more specific and accurate. There are a variety of filters such as –

c. Country – Two letter country code (Ex: IN)
d. Net – specific IP Range or Subnet
e. OS – Operating System
f. Port – Specific Ports
g. City – Find devices in a specified city.
h. Geo – you can pass its geographical coordinates, etc.

Example – Apache Country:IN

This will show results for Apache service with the country code specified.

Steps to use Shodan Search

a. Visit www.shodan.io
b. In Search Box input the search query according to a specific target. For Example: we want to look for apache services in Jaipur City. We will use the following filter –

```
Apache city:"Jaipur"
```

c. The results shown will look like as described in the below image.

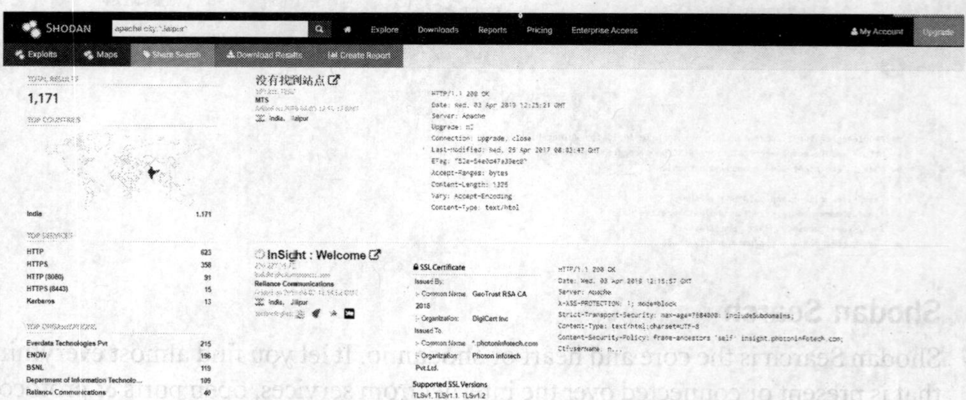

d. Select any of the search results to get an in-depth report.

The common Shodan search results include the following information –

a. Geographical Information
b. Organization & ISP
c. Hostname
d. Services
e. Open Ports
f. Web Technologies
g. Vulnerabilities that may occur

h. SSL Certificate Information
i. Banner Information, Etc.

Shodan Explore

Shodan Explore is also a similar feature to search but it let you look for common search results, top votes targets and give finding like –

a. Industrial control systems
b. Webcams
c. Routers
d. Traffic Lights
e. Other IoT Devices & Credentials, etc.

Using Shodan Explore

a. Visit www.shodan.io
b. Click on **Explore** button adjacent to Shodan search bar.
c. It will show options like Featured Categories, Top Voted Queries, Recently Shared, etc. (Refer to the image below):

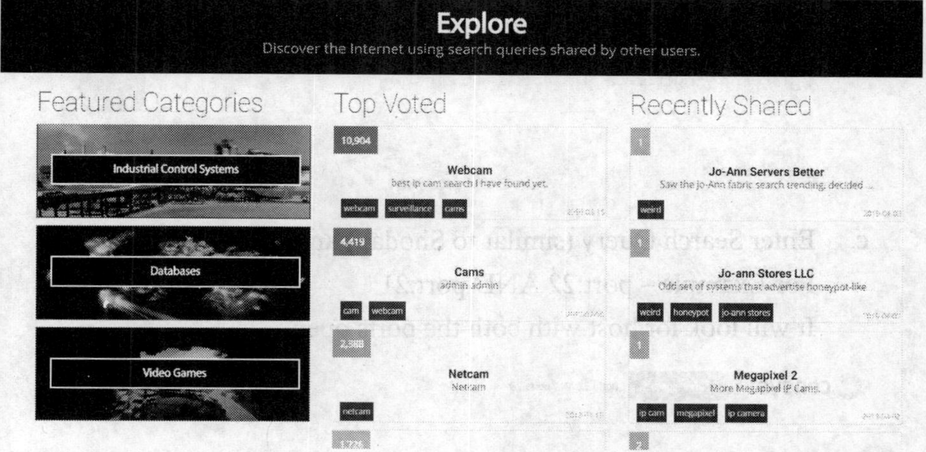

d. Click on any option to show results and detail information as done in Shodan Search Option.

Advance Shodan Usage

There is various advance usage of Shodan which can be self-explore after consistent practice. Some of the advance usages are –

a. **Data Export** allows exporting results in various formats.
b. **Browser Search** allows to configuring shodan search from the URL bar.

Censys – Mapping the Internet

Censys.io is yet another important tool like Shodan, which is used to find every possible device whether exposed, vulnerable or secure (ensures visibility on internet).

According to Censys.io, Security starts with visibility. It helps you to find and monitor almost every server on the Internet. The intel retrieved from the monitor and analysis of the devices on the internet can be helpful for securing your organization or business from threats, create datasets for research and analysis, etc.

Steps to use Censys.io

a. Visit www.censys.io

b. Perform search under **What servers & devices are exposed on my network?** Moreover, the search can be performed in the three following areas –

- IP Address (IPv4 Hosts)
- Website Address
- Certificate

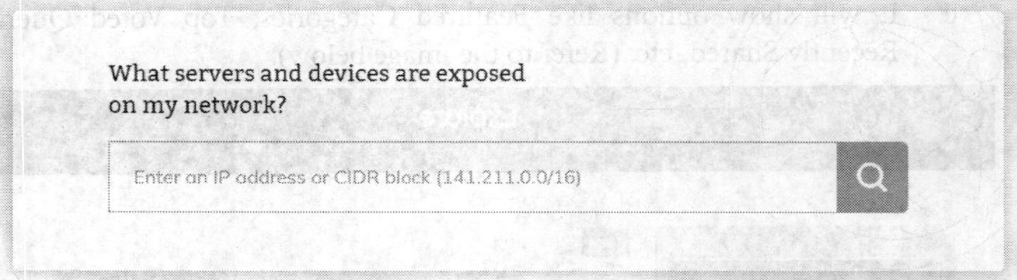

c. Enter Search Query (similar to Shodan) and click on Search Icon.

For Example – port:22 AND port:21

It will look for host with both the ports open.

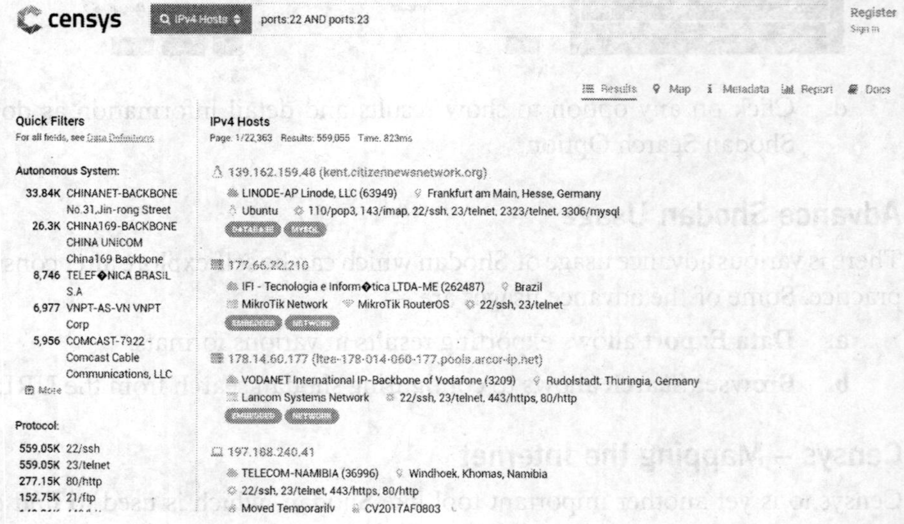

d. Select a search result to view detailed report.

CyberChef – The Cyber Swiss Army Knife

CyberChef is a simple modern web application which can be used for analysis, encoding/decoding data without interacting with complex algorithms, programming languages or tools. It is easy to use and can be understood by both technical & non-technical people.

According to CyberChef, there are around 200 useful operations in CyberChef for anyone working on anything vaguely Internet-related, whether you just want to convert a timestamp to a different format, decompress gzipped data, create a SHA3 hash, or parse an X.509 certificate to find out who issued it. It is expected that CyberChef will be useful for cybersecurity and antivirus companies. It should also appeal to the academic world and any individuals or companies involved in the analysis of digital data, be that software developers, analysts, mathematicians or casual puzzle solvers.

Keyboard Shortcuts (Key bindings)

Command	Shortcut (Win/Linux)	Shortcut (Mac)
Place cursor in search field	Ctrl+Alt+f	Ctrl+Opt+f
Place cursor in input box	Ctrl+Alt+i	Ctrl+Opt+i
Place cursor in output box	Ctrl+Alt+o	Ctrl+Opt+o
Place cursor in first argument field of the next operation in the recipe	Ctrl+Alt+.	Ctrl+Opt+.
Place cursor in first argument field of the nth operation in the recipe	Ctrl+Alt+[1-9]	Ctrl+Opt+[1-9]
Disable current operation	Ctrl+Alt+d	Ctrl+Opt+d
Set/clear breakpoint	Ctrl+Alt+b	Ctrl+Opt+b
Bake	Ctrl+Alt+Space	Ctrl+Opt+Space
Step	Ctrl+Alt+'	Ctrl+Opt+'
Clear recipe	Ctrl+Alt+c	Ctrl+Opt+c
Save to file	Ctrl+Alt+s	Ctrl+Opt+s
Load recipe	Ctrl+Alt+l	Ctrl+Opt+l
Move output to input	Ctrl+Alt+m	Ctrl+Opt+m

Tools Provided by CyberChef

a. **Data Formats** such as Hex, Base64, Binary, Octal, Decimal, etc.

b. **Encryption/Encoding** such as AES, DES, Bowlfish, RC2, RC4, Enigma, Bombe, etc.

c. **Public Key** such as PEM to Hex, Hex to PEM, PGP Encrypt & Decrypt, etc.

d. **Arithmetic Logic, Networking, Forensics and variety of tools to explore.**

e. We will look at some of the tools of CyberChef and rest of the tools can be self-explored after little practice and understanding.

To use CyberChef Visit – https://gchq.github.io/CyberChef/

A. Base 64 Encoding/Decoding

Base64 is a notation for encoding arbitrary byte data using a restricted set of symbols that can be conveniently used by humans and processed by computers. (Source – Cyberchef)

1. *Base 64 Encoding*
    a. Open CyberChef & Drag **To Base 64** under Favourites or Data Format Menu and Drop it under **Recipe Section.**
    b. Under the Recipe Section, you can choose different Base64 Algorithm, by default standard is set.
    c. By default, **Auto Bake** is enabled which dynamically reflect changes in output for provided input if Recipe is changed. You can untick Auto Bake & do it manually as well.
    d. Under Input Section, provide a string to encode.
    e. You will get a Base64 encoded string under Output section.
    f. Refer to below image to understand the whole process.

```
Here, Input is - Hi I am Harsh
Output is - SGkgSSBhbSBIYXJzaA==
```

2. *Base64 Decoding*
    a. Open CyberChef & Drag **From Base 64** under Favourites or Data Format Menu and Drop it under the **Recipe Section.**
    b. Under the Recipe Section, you can choose different Base64 Algorithm, by default standard is set.
    c. By default **Auto Bake** is enabled which dynamically reflect changes in the output for provided input if Recipe is changed. You can untick Auto Bake & do it manually as well.
    d. Under Input Section, provide Base64 string to decode.
    e. You will get a Plain-Text string under the Output section.
    f. Refer to below image to understand the whole process.

```
Here, Input is - SGkgSSBhbSBIYXJzaA==
The Output is - Hi I am Harsh
```

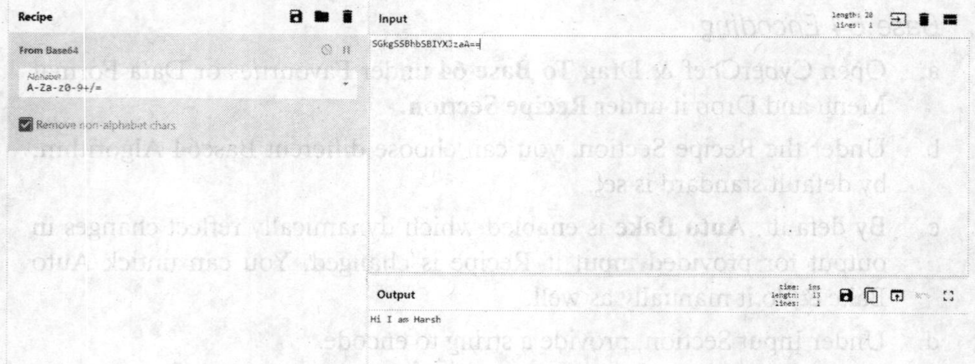

B. AES Encryption/Decryption

Advanced Encryption Standard (AES) is a U.S. Federal Information Processing Standard (FIPS). It was selected after a 5-year process where 15 competing designs were evaluated.

Key: The following algorithms will be used based on the size of the key:

16 bytes = AES-128

24 bytes = AES-192

32 bytes = AES-256

You can generate a password-based key using one of the KDF operations.

IV: The Initialization Vector should be 16 bytes long. If not entered, it will default to 16 null bytes.

Padding: In CBC and ECB mode, PKCS#7 padding will be used.

GCM Tag: This field is ignored unless 'GCM' mode is used & it is used while decryption.

(Source – CyberChef)

AES Encryption

a. Open CyberChef & Drag **AES Encrypt** present under Encoding/ Encryption Menu and Drop it under **Recipe Section.**
b. Under the Recipe Section, provide **Key & IV.** (According to standard size & IV is optional)
c. By default, **Auto Bake** is enabled which dynamically reflect changes in output for provided input if Recipe is changed. You can untick Auto Bake & do it manually as well.
d. Under Input Section, provide a plain-text string to encode
e. You will get an AES Encrypted string under the Output section.
f. Refer to below image to understand the whole process.

```
Key - AESEEEEEEEEEEEEEEEEEEEEEeSSESESESSESESESE
IV - ADFJLJFLJSLKJFLKJLSKFJLKJSFLKJSFKLJFLSKJK
Input - Hi I am Harsh
Output - 83ebaeaf5d15f49564e9937f81694300
```

Follow similar steps for AES Decryption, Instead of AES Encrypt, select AES Decrypt & Provide AES String as Input.

```
Key - AESEEEEEEEEEEEEEEEEEEEEEeSSESESESSESESESE
IV - ADFJLJFLJSLKJFLKJLSKFJLKJSFLKJSFKLJFLSKJK
Input - 83ebaeaf5d15f49564e9937f81694300
Output - Hi I am Harsh
```

C. *Hex to PEM*

Converts a hexadecimal DER (Distinguished Encoding Rules) string into PEM (Privacy Enhanced Mail) format. (source – CyberChef)

a. Open CyberChef & Drag **Hex to PEM** present under Public Key Menu and Drop it under **Recipe Section.**
b. Under the Recipe Section, provide **Header String.**
c. By default, **Auto Bake** is enabled which dynamically reflect changes in output for provided input if Recipe is changed. You can untick Auto Bake & do it manually as well.
d. Under Input Section, provide a HEX to convert into PEM.
e. You will get a PEM string under the Output section.
f. Refer to below image to understand the whole process. (example shows the use of plain text.)

```
Header String - HARSH
Input - Hi I am Harsh
Output - -----BEGIN HARSH-----
AAAKAKA=
-----END HARSH-----
```

D. *Generate QR Code*

Generates a Quick Response (QR) code from the input text.

A QR code is a type of matrix barcode (or two-dimensional barcode) first designed in 1994 for the automotive industry in Japan. A barcode is a machine-readable optical label that contains information about the item to which it is attached. *(Source – Cyberchef)*

a. Open CyberChef & Drag **Generate QR Code** present under **Other** Menu and Drop it under **Recipe Section.**

b. Under the Recipe Section, provide arguments *i.e.* Image Format, Module Size, Margin & Error Correction.

c. By default, **Auto Bake** is enabled which dynamically reflect changes in output for provided input if Recipe is changed. You can untick Auto Bake & do it manually as well.

d. Under Input Section, provide a Plain-Text String to get a QR Code.

e. You will get an QR Code under the Output section.

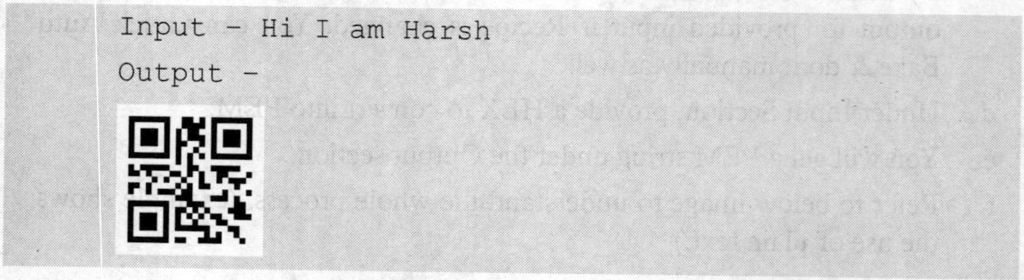

There are tons of other tools present in CyberChef which are worth spending time and explore. It is highly recommended to practice each of them. They are sometime useful while playing capture the flags, doing investigations or performing a penetration test. With practice you will get in-depth understanding of each & every tool.

FOCA – Fingerprinting Organizations with Collected Archives

FOCA is one of the most popular and widely used tools by Information Security Researchers to find hidden information, metadata and other details from documents. The documents can be present anywhere such as remote servers or web pages.

According to FOCA, It is capable of analysing a wide variety of documents, with the most common being Microsoft Office, Open Office, or PDF files, although it also analyses Adobe InDesign or SVG files, for instance. These documents are searched for using three possible search engines: Google, Bing, and DuckDuckGo. The sum of the results from the three engines amounts to many of documents. It is also possible to add local files to extract the EXIF information from graphic files, and a complete analysis of the information discovered through the URL is conducted even before downloading the file.

It has the following major functionalities such as –

a. DNS Search
b. Web Search
c. IP Resolution
d. Robtex
e. DNS Prediction
f. Bing IP
g. Metadata Extraction
h. Network Analysis
i. Fingerprinting
j. Backup Search
k. Leaks & Technology Identification, etc.

Steps to use FOCA

a. Download FOCA (https://filehippo.com/download_foca/) and Install it.
b. Start FOCA & Add a New Project. To Add New Project, Click on Project Menu > New Project & Fill required details like Project Name, Domain Website, etc. (Refer to the image below)

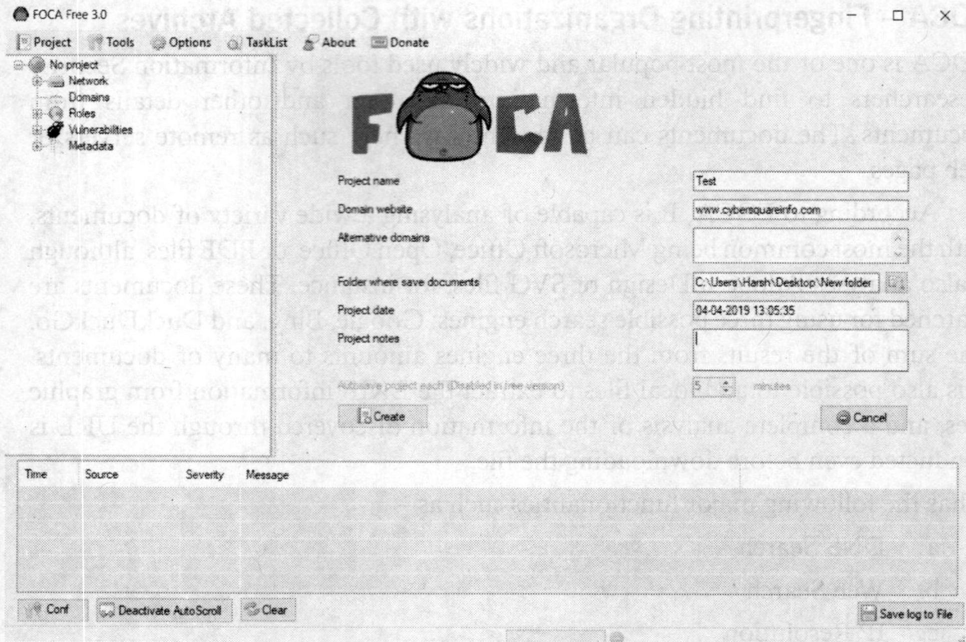

c. In the left sidebar, as shown in the above image, there are various options such as Network and Metadata. By click upon them, you can use different search and scan type.

d. Click on Network & select scans you want to perform such as Web Searcher, DNS Search, etc. (if you will click on any scan, it will be deselected) & click on Start.

e. If there are multiple IPs, you can skip to next IP at any step.

f. Under Roles, you can crawl various options & look for information gathered from the scan. In this example, we can get DNS Information. It depends upon your nature of scan that what kind of information will be reflected.

g. Refer to the below image which indicates the ongoing scan using FOCA.

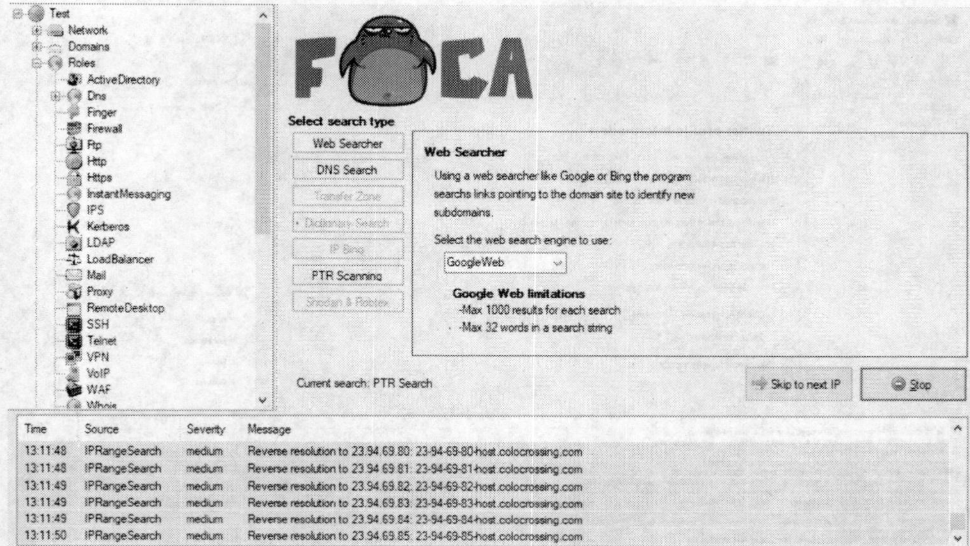

Creepy – Geolocation OSINT Tool

Creepy is a useful and handy Geolocation based OSINT Tool which is highly useful in mastering Information Gathering & crawling useful data.

According to Creepy, It gathers geolocation related information from online sources and allows for presentation on the map, search filtering based on the exact location and/or date, export in csv format or kml for further analysis in Google Maps.

Download & Install Creepy - https://www.geocreepy.com/

Quick Start Instructions (provided by geocreepy.com)

a. Download creepy (source code or the installers provided here for your platform)

b. Configure the plugins. Edit → Plugins Configuration → Select plugin and run the wizards, following the instructions.

c. Create a new project: Creepy → New Project → Person Based Project. Search for the target selecting the available plugins.

d. Right click on the project → Analyze Current Project

e. Wait

f. The locations will be drawn on the map, once the analysis is complete.

g. Filter locations, export locations, view them on the map.

Refer to below image for sample search & results.

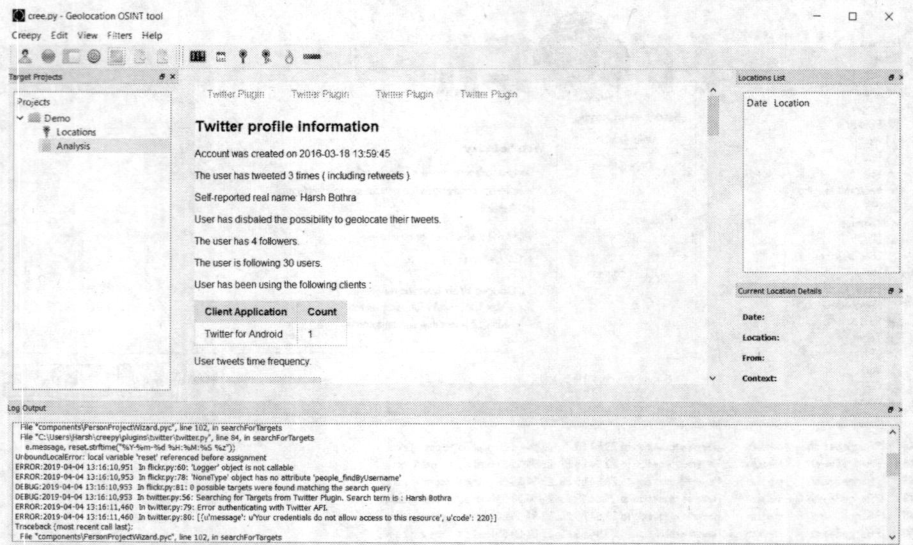

You can perform a search using single or multiple plugins, in the above example, the only Twitter plugin is used, but due to lack of geolocation information, the map is not drawn. The result depends upon the nature of target, search & plugins used.

Dmitry – Deep Magic Information Gathering Tool

Dmitry is one of the simplest and basic information gathering tool, which is easy to use but can get much of useful piece of information. It comes pre-installed in Kali Linux. We will use Kali Linux to learn about Dmitry.

Step for using Dmitry

a. Boot Kali Linux VM.

b. Open Kali Linux Terminal & type **dmitry.** It will output **Dmitry** tool with basic usage information.

```
root@kali:~# dmitry
Deepmagic Information Gathering Tool
"There be some deep magic going on"
Usage: dmitry [-winsepfb] [-t 0-9] [-o %host.txt]
host
  -o  Save output to %host.txt or to file
      specified by -o file
  -i  Perform a whois lookup on the IP address of
      a host
  -w  Perform a whois lookup on the domain name of
      a host
  -n  Retrieve Netcraft.com information on a host
  -s  Perform a search for possible subdomains
```

```
  -e   Perform a search for possible email
       addresses
  -p   Perform a TCP port scan on a host
* -f   Perform a TCP port scan on a host showing
       output reporting filtered ports
* -b   Read in the banner received from the scanned
       port
* -t 0-9 Set the TTL in seconds when scanning a
       TCP port (Default 2)
*Requires the -p flagged to be passed
<end of command>
```

c. we will look at one example for information gathering which involves whois lookup for Domain name & IP of a host & Subdomain.

```
Command - dimtry -wis www.cybersquareinfo.com -o
abc.txt
root@kali:~# dmitry -wis www.cybersquareinfo.com
Deepmagic Information Gathering Tool
"There be some deep magic going on"
HostIP:23.94.69.34
HostName:www.cybersquareinfo.com
Gathered Inet-whois information for 23.94.69.34
---------------------------------
inetnum:        23.83.128.0 - 23.105.223.255
netname:        NON-RIPE-NCC-MANAGED-ADDRESS-BLOCK
descr:          IPv4 address block not managed by
the RIPE NCC
...
...
...
country:        EU # Country is really world wide
admin-c:        IANA1-RIPE
tech-c:         IANA1-RIPE
status:         ALLOCATED UNSPECIFIED
mnt-by:         RIPE-NCC-HM-MNT
created:        2019-01-07T10:48:39Z
remarks:        For more information on IANA
services
remarks:        go to IANA web site at http://www.
iana.org.
% This query was served by the RIPE Database Query
Service version 1.93.2 (ANGUS)
Gathered Inic-whois information for
cybersquareinfo.com
```

```
---------------------------------
    Domain Name: CYBERSQUAREINFO.COM
    Registry Domain ID: 2142288271_DOMAIN_COM-VRSN
    Registrar WHOIS Server: whois.godaddy.com
    Registrar URL: http://www.godaddy.com
    Updated Date: 2018-06-26T17:03:01Z
    Creation Date: 2017-07-11T19:09:31Z
      ...
      ...
      ...
    Domain Status: clientTransferProhibited
https://icann.org/epp#clientTransferProhibited
    Domain Status: clientUpdateProhibited https://
icann.org/epp#clientUpdateProhibited
    Name Server: ULTRA-ONE.BASEZAP.COM
    Name Server: ULTRA-TWO.BASEZAP.COM
    DNSSEC: unsigned
    URL of the ICANN Whois Inaccuracy Complaint
Form: https://www.icann.org/wicf/
      ...
      ...
      ...
Gathered Subdomain information for
cybersquareinfo.com
---------------------------------
Searching Google.com:80...
Found 0 possible subdomain(s) for host
cybersquareinfo.com, Searched 0 pages containing 0
results
All scans completed, exiting
<End of Command>
```

There are various other parameters which can be used in combination in similar fashion according to the requirement, it is good practice to explore it tool a bit and create cheat sheet/note down some combinations for various case scenarios which can be used directly as and when required, it not only saves the time but boosts the process as well.

Sublist3r – Subdomain Discovery Tool

Sublist3r is an open source python-based tool which is used for subdomain discovery and traversal. Subdomains plays a vital role while testing a target. In many cases, a subdomain is vulnerable and can be compromised, sometimes a subdomain takeover leads to complete domain takeover further. It crawls and looks for information in various public domains & search engines such as Google, Yahoo, Bing, Baidu, etc.

It allows functionality to brute force sub domains for given domain with integrate tool **subbrute.**

Sublist3r doesn't come pre-installed with kali Linux, we need to clone it from GitHub and do the necessary housekeeping before able to use the tool. The concepts of git and GitHub, we learned in initial part of the book will be useful now.

Installing Sublist3r in Kali Linux

a. Open Terminal & Clone Sublist3r repository from GitHub using following command –

```
git clone https://github.com/aboul3la/Sublist3r
```

b. Move to Sublist3r directory with following command –

```
cd Sublist3r
```

c. Since, there are various modules used in the tool which might not present in your kali Linux environment it is required to install those required packages. There is a requirement file which contains the data for packages required and can be used to install packages using package installer for python PIP.

```
pip install -r requirement.txt
```

d. Now, Sublist3r is ready to use. You can run help command to view various options available in Sublist3r.

```
python sublist3r.py -h
```

Steps to use Sublist3r for Subdomain Discovery

a. Run following command for simple subdomain discovery.

```
python sublist3r.py -d <domain_name>
(here -d represent domain flag.)
root@kali:~/Sublist3r# python sublist3r.py -d
google.com -e netcraft
[-] Enumerating subdomains now for google.com
[-] Searching now in Netcraft..
[-] Total Unique Subdomains Found: 195
www.google.com
aboutme.google.com
accounts.google.com
admin.google.com
...
...
```

```
...
vr.google.com
wallet.google.com
wap.google.com
webmaster.google.com
whois.google.com
work.google.com
ww.google.com
<end of command>
```

b. Run following command for subdomain discovery with brute force.

```
root@kali:~/Sublist3r# python sublist3r.py -d
google.com -e netcraft -b -t 50
[-] Enumerating subdomains now for google.com
[-] Searching now in Netcraft..
[-] Starting bruteforce module now using
subbrute..
<end of command>
```

Recon-ng – Reconnaissance Framework

Recon-ng is one of the great Recon tools which is widely used by information security professionals. This tool is developed by Tim Tomes at Black Hills Information Security.

It is a reconnaissance tool having a similar interface like Metasploit framework and can be directly used using command line interface. Recon-ng comes pre-installed with kali linux or else can be configured & installed using following command –

```
sudo apt-get install recon-ng
```

Using Recon-ng

a. Boot Kali Linux & Open Terminal

b. Use following command to start recon-ng:

```
recon-ng
root@kali:~# recon-ng
. . .
. . .
[75] Recon modules
[8]  Reporting modules
[2]  Import modules
[2]  Exploitation modules
[2]  Discovery modules
[recon-ng][default] >
<end of command>
```

c. The above command shows recon-ng terminal output which has several different options. To use recon-ng we need to use various commands. To watch commands, use following after getting to above screen. Refer to below image.

```
Commands (type [help|?] <topic>):
---------------------------------
add             Adds records to the database
back            Exits the current context
delete          Deletes records from the database
exit            Exits the framework
help            Displays this menu
keys            Manages framework API keys
load            Loads specified module
pdb             Starts a Python Debugger session
query           Queries the database
record          Records commands to a resource file
reload          Reloads all modules
resource        Executes commands from a resource file
search          Searches available modules
set             Sets module options
shell           Executes shell commands
show            Shows various framework items
snapshots       Manages workspace snapshots
spool           Spools output to a file
unset           Unsets module options
use             Loads specified module
workspaces      Manages workspaces
```

d. To check all the available modules present in recon-ng, use following command –

```
[recon-ng][default] > show modules
```

```
[recon-ng][default] > show modules

  Discovery
  ---------
    discovery/info_disclosure/cache_snoop
    discovery/info_disclosure/interesting_files

  Exploitation
  ------------
    exploitation/injection/command_injector
    exploitation/injection/xpath_bruter

  Import
  ------
    import/csv_file
    import/list

  Recon
  -----
    recon/companies-contacts/bing_linkedin_cache
    recon/companies-contacts/jigsaw/point_usage
    recon/companies-contacts/jigsaw/purchase_contact
    recon/companies-contacts/jigsaw/search_contacts
    recon/companies-multi/github_miner
    recon/companies-multi/whois_miner
    recon/contacts-contacts/mailtester
    recon/contacts-contacts/mangle
    recon/contacts-contacts/unmangle
    recon/contacts-credentials/hibp_breach
    recon/contacts-credentials/hibp_paste
    recon/contacts-domains/migrate_contacts
    recon/contacts-profiles/fullcontact
    recon/credentials-credentials/adobe
    recon/credentials-credentials/bozocrack
    recon/credentials-credentials/hashes_org
```

e. recon-ng integrates various third-party tools using API Integrations, you can check the list of API Keys with following command (to use a particular tool, you need to have its API key for its working) –

```
[recon-ng][default] > keys list
```

f. To add an API key, use following command –

```
[recon-ng][default] > keys add <api_service> <api_key>
```

```
[recon-ng][default] > keys list

  +----------------------------+
  |       Name        | Value |
  +----------------------------+
  | bing_api          |       |
  | builtwith_api     |       |
  | censysio_id       |       |
  | censysio_secret   |       |
  | flickr_api        |       |
  | fullcontact_api   |       |
  | github_api        |       |
  | google_api        |       |
  | google_cse        |       |
  | hashes_api        |       |
  | ipinfodb_api      |       |
  | jigsaw_api        |       |
  | jigsaw_password   |       |
  | jigsaw_username   |       |
  | pwnedlist_api     |       |
  | pwnedlist_iv      |       |
  | pwnedlist_secret  |       |
  | shodan_api        |       |
  | twitter_api       |       |
  | twitter_secret    |       |
  +----------------------------+

[recon-ng][default] > keys add shodan_api 1234353
[*] Key 'shodan_api' added.
```

g. To use any module in recon-ng, first of all check the module name and then select module using following command –

```
[recon-ng][default] > use <module_name>
```

For Example:

```
[recon-ng][default] > use discovery/info_disclosure/interesting_files
```

Once the module is loaded, use show info command to check various information about module and input required to be set for the tool.

```
[recon-ng][default] > use discovery/info_disclosure/interesting_files
[recon-ng][default][interesting_files] > show info

      Name: Interesting File Finder
      Path: modules/discovery/info_disclosure/interesting_files.py
    Author: Tim Tomes (@LaNMaSteR53), thrapt (thrapt@gmail.com), Jay Turla (@shipcod3), and Mark Jeffery

Description:
  Checks hosts for interesting files in predictable locations.

Options:
  Name      Current Value  Required  Description
  --------  -------------  --------  -----------
  DOWNLOAD  True           yes       download discovered files
  PORT      80             yes       request port
  PROTOCOL  http           yes       request protocol
  SOURCE    default        yes       source of input (see 'show info' for details)

Source Options:
  default        SELECT DISTINCT host FROM hosts WHERE host IS NOT NULL
  <string>       string representing a single input
  <path>         path to a file containing a list of inputs
  query <sql>    database query returning one column of inputs
```

h. for above example, set source (target) using following command – **set source <source>**

i. To perform the scan use, **run** command.

```
[recon-ng][default][interesting_files] > set source www.cybersquareinfo.com
SOURCE => www.cybersquareinfo.com
[recon-ng][default][interesting_files] > run
[*] http://www.cybersquareinfo.com:80/robots.txt => Error
[*] http://www.cybersquareinfo.com:80/sitemap.xml => Error
[*] http://www.cybersquareinfo.com:80/sitemap.xml.gz => Error
[*] http://www.cybersquareinfo.com:80/crossdomain.xml => Error
[*] http://www.cybersquareinfo.com:80/phpinfo.php => Error
[*] http://www.cybersquareinfo.com:80/test.php => Error
[*] http://www.cybersquareinfo.com:80/elmah.axd => Error
[*] http://www.cybersquareinfo.com:80/server-status => Error
[*] http://www.cybersquareinfo.com:80/jmx-console/ => Error
[*] http://www.cybersquareinfo.com:80/admin-console/ => Error
[*] http://www.cybersquareinfo.com:80/web-console/ => Error
[*] 0 interesting files found.
[*] ...downloaded to '/root/.recon-ng/workspaces/default/'
[recon-ng][default][interesting_files] >
```

There are over 80 tools in recon-ng, some of which requires API Keys to be integrated externally. You can self-explore each of the module easily. Every module has working description and requirement to guide you through it. It is highly recommended to spend as much as possible time on recon-ng to practice it & you will be able to master various information gathering tools.

P0f – Passive Recon Tool

P0f is one of the interest passive recon tool which let you determine the potential target's operating system without directly interacting or touching it physically as well as logically. That's the speciality of this tool.

Since, each operating system implements TCP/IP Stacks differently (Different RFC Code Implementations), that's why the packets transmitted through different operating system may slightly vary in attributes. By capturing the packet and examining it thoroughly we can determine the target operating system with enhanced accuracy. To understand this tool, it is recommended to revise concepts of TCP/IP explained in networking chapter.

Determining Operating System with P0f

a. Boot Kali Linux & Open Terminal.
b. use following command to run P0f

```
p0f -i <interface>
For Example - p0f -i eth0
```

c. Open web browser and browse any website to generate some traffic & p0f will start capturing the packets & data will be shown in terminal as shown below –

```
root@kali:~# p0f -i eth0
--- p0f 3.09b by Michal Zalewski <lcamtuf@
coredump.cx> ---
[+] Closed 1 file descriptor.
[+] Loaded 322 signatures from '/etc/p0f/p0f.fp'.
[+] Intercepting traffic on interface 'eth0'.
[+] Default packet filtering configured [+VLAN].
[+] Entered main event loop.
.-[ 192.168.121.137/59786 -> 23.48.201.32/80 (syn)
]-
|
| client    = 192.168.121.137/59786
| os        = Linux 3.11 and newer
| dist      = 0
| params    = none
|raw_sig=
4:64+0:0:1460:mss*20,7:mss,sok,ts,nop,ws:df,id+:0
|
`----
.-[ 192.168.121.137/59786 -> 23.48.201.32/80 (mtu)
]-
|
| client    = 192.168.121.137/59786
| link      = Ethernet or modem
| raw_mtu   = 1500
|
`----
. . .
. . .
. . .
```

```
^C[!] WARNING: User-initiated shutdown.
All done. Processed 359 packets.
<end of command>
```

As you can see, the highlighted text in output contains the OS which is Linux 3.11 & newer & we have used Kali Linux, this signifies the target OS determination using this tool. Also notice, before end of command, when we manually exited the tool, it already processed more than 359 packets.

This is very easy and handy tool to use but requires good understanding of networking concepts especially TCP/IP.

Sparta – A Recon Tool

Sparta is a GUI based python tool which integrates some popular tools in single script and some of them are:

a. Nmap
b. Hydra
c. Nikto
d. CutyCapt
e. Netcat
f. Snmp-enum & Snmp-check, etc.

This tool comes pre-installed with latest versions of Kali Linux and for other operating systems, it can be downloaded and configured according to OS Requirements.

Using Sparta for Reconnaissance

a. Boot Kali Linux & Open Terminal.
b. To start Sparta, use the following command

```
root@kali:~# sparta
[+] Creating temporary files..
[+] Wordlist was created/opened: /tmp/sparta-XUA4mP-tool-output/sparta-usernames.txt
[+] Wordlist was created/opened: /tmp/sparta-XUA4mP-tool-output/sparta-passwords.txt
[+] Loading settings file..
```

It will open Sparta GUI & above output will be shown in terminal as backend process.

c. Under Scan → Host → Click to add host(s) to scope. It will prompt a window asking for IP Address or Range of IPs to scan & you can also provide CIDR notation to scan entire subnet of provided range.

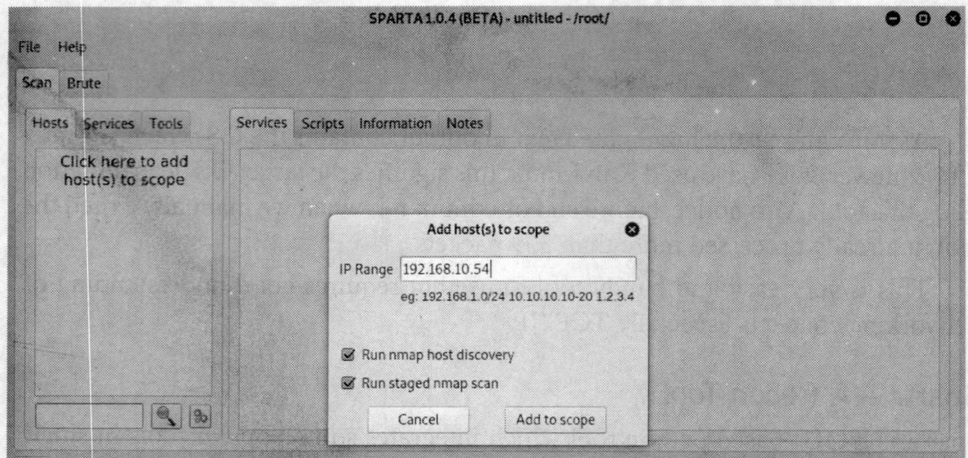

d. After adding to scope, Sparta will start scanning in various stages.

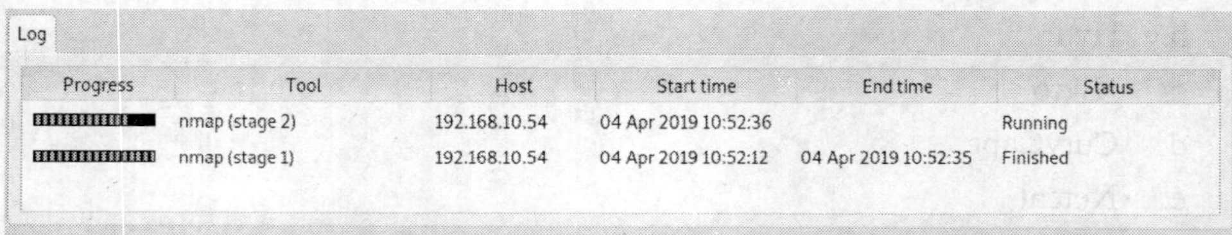

e. After finishing the process, it will show the various results as shown below.

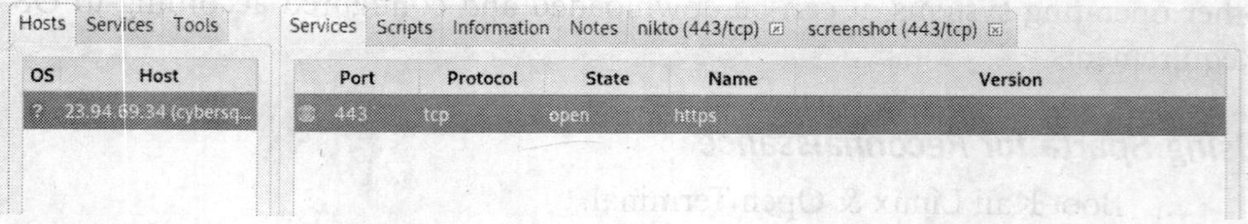

f. To get more additional information, click on **Information Tab**. Also, you can check various port information under **Nikto Tab.**

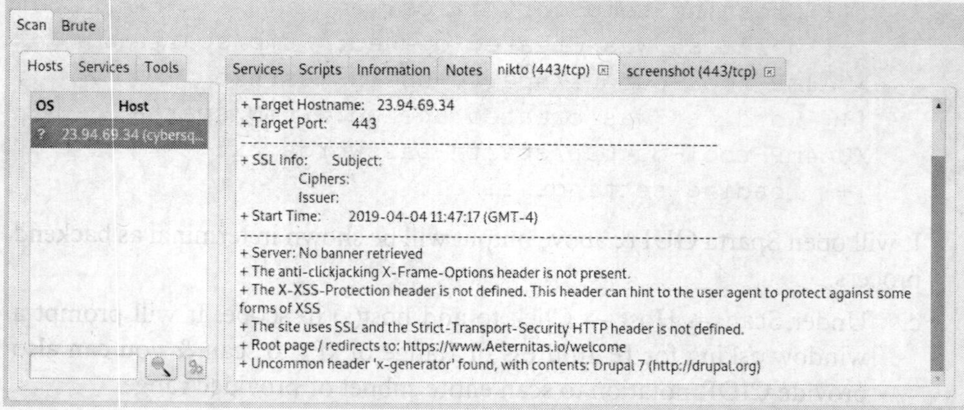

g. Under **Tools Section**, there are various tools which can be used for the specified target.

h. This tool also provides brute-force capabilities using Hydra. For this you need to go under **Brute Force Tab** & specify port, IP and service to perform brute force.

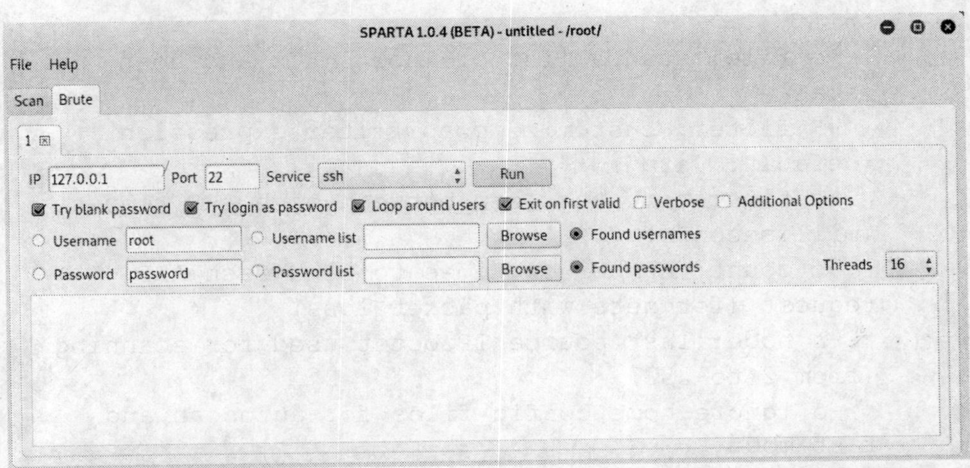

This tool makes the whole information gathering process easier and increases the accessibility & saves time by integrating almost every useful tool under single entity.

Netdiscover – Live Host Identification Tool

Netdiscover is a simple utility which facilitates capabilities of ARP Scanning to identify live hosts in the network or subnet. It is a very handy tool for initial recon purposes. It provides various features such as:

a. ARP Scanner
b. Multiple Subnet Scanning
c. Live Display of Output
d. Active & Passive Mode, Etc.

Host Discovery & Identification with Netdiscover

a. Boot Kali Linux & Open Terminal.
b. use following command to run netdiscover & check list of available options:

```
root@kali:~# netdiscover -h
Written by: Jaime Penalba <jpenalbae@gmail.com>
Usage: netdiscover [-i device] [-r range | -l file
| -p] [-m file] [-F filter] [-s time] [-c count]
[-n node] [-dfPLNS]
  -i device: your network device
  -r range: scan a given range instead of auto
scan. 192.168.6.0/24,/16,/8
```

```
  -l file: scan the list of ranges contained into
the given file
  -p passive mode: do not send anything, only
sniff
  -m file: scan a list of known MACs and host
names
  -F filter: customize pcap filter expression
(default: "arp")
  -s time: time to sleep between each ARP request
(milliseconds)
  -c count: number of times to send each ARP
request (for nets with packet loss)
  -n node: last source IP octet used for scanning
(from 2 to 253)
  -d ignore home config files for autoscan and
fast mode
  -f enable fastmode scan, saves a lot of time,
recommended for auto
  -P print results in a format suitable for
parsing by another program and stop after active
scan
  -L similar to -P but continue listening after
the active scan is completed
  -N Do not print header. Only valid when -P or -L
is enabled.
  -S enable sleep time suppression between each
request (hardcore mode)
If -r, -l or -p are not enabled, netdiscover will
scan for common LAN addresses.
<end of command>
```

c. now to perform passive scanning using netdiscover, perform following command

```
netdiscover -p -r <ip_range>
```

```
root@kali: ~
File  Edit  View  Search  Terminal  Help
Currently scanning: (passive)   |   Screen View: Unique Hosts

11 Captured ARP Req/Rep packets, from 2 hosts.   Total size: 660
 IP            At MAC Address     Count     Len  MAC Vendor / Hostname
-----------------------------------------------------------------------
192.168.121.1  00:50:56:c0:00:08      9     540  VMware, Inc.
192.168.121.2  00:50:56:f4:73:67      2     120  VMware, Inc.
```

There are various options which can be used according to the problem scenario. It is a good practice to work and learn about various options present in this tool which can be easily self-explored.

Maltego

Maltego is a great tool for Data Mining, Visualization & Information and Intel Research. It is one of the top tools used by security researchers. Maltego is capable of extracting intel about the network or even an individual. It is proprietary software developed by Patevra.

It provides a library of transforms which can be used for discovery and extraction of intel from various public and open sources, visualize them and perform mining operations. The basic focus behind this tool is to build a relationship between entities representing real world connections.

What can Maltego do?

It can perform various data mining & visualization to create and predict real world relationships between –

- Individuals or Groups
- Companies & Organizations
- Web Applications & Remote Servers
- Domains
- IP addresses & Netblocks
- Documents and files, etc.

Maltego is a cross-platform, easy to install tool which can be used on Windows, Mac & Linux with support of Java Dependencies. (It requires java to run)

It comes in various editions ranging from commercial (enterprise) to community editions. Kali Linux has Maltego pre-installed. Prior to use, it is recommended to create an account for using it. You will need this account to login and after that you will be able to work with Maltego. You can simply create account on https://www.paterva.com/web7/community/community.php just like any other social media or email account setup.

Please note that if you are using system with low configurations, it is recommended to turn off or suspend unnecessary process, else it may result into system hanging or Maltego and even system may crash.

As we discussed, Maltego is an interactive Data Mining tool which renders directed graphs for relationship analysis. There are some terminologies associated with Maltego that you need to know are –

- Entity – Represented as a node on graph & can be anything such as a DNS Name, Person, Phone, etc.
- Transform – Piece of code that takes one entity to another.
- Machines – Chain Multiple Transforms together to automate common/ tedious task.

Using Maltego

(you can use terminal as well)

a. Wait for a moment till it finishes initial loading & a prompt screen will ask for registration. If you haven't registered yourself, create an account following the hyperlink & come back to login. & Choose Community Edition (CE).

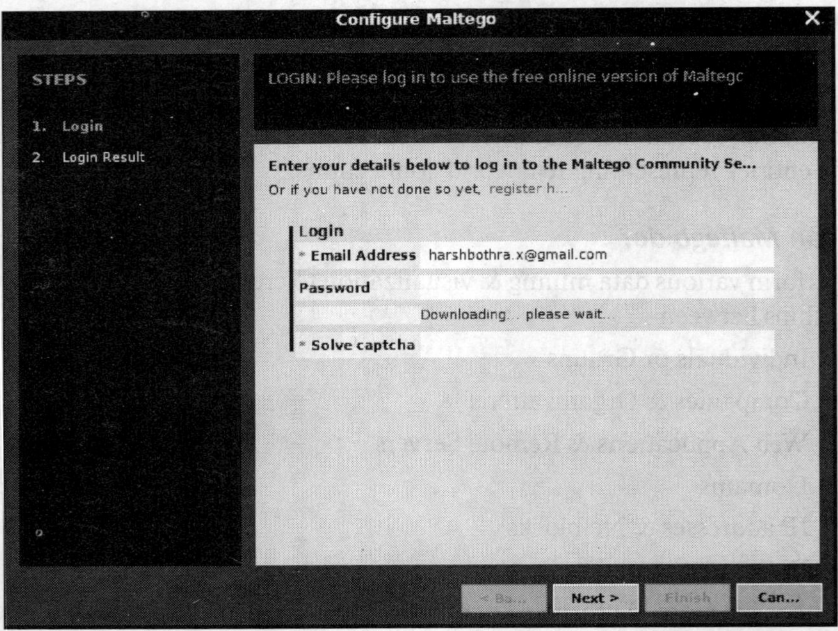

b. Maltego works on transformation, so install all the required transformation with **Transformation Hub.** Some of the transformations may require APIs to work while some are present online for commercial editions. Refer to below image for how transformations hub looks like.

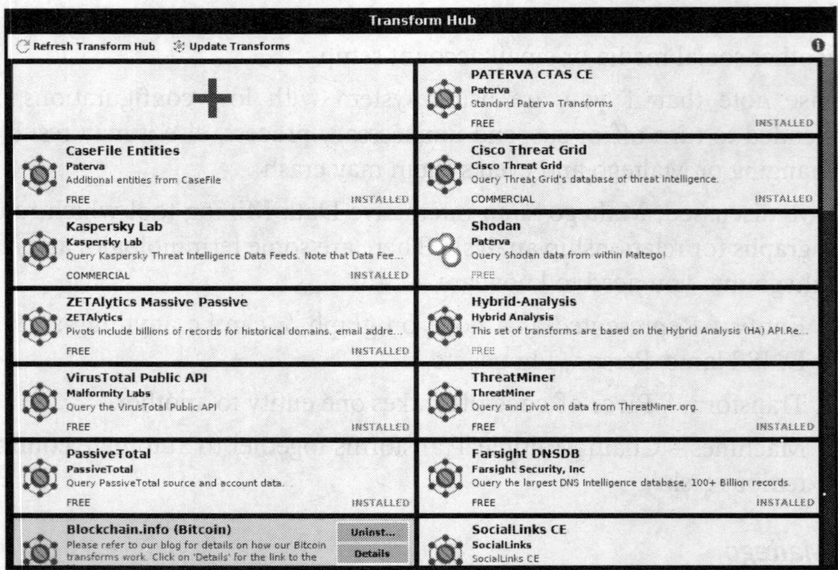

c. Create a new graph (new project) by pressing **Ctrl+T or Cmd+T**. This will open a blank graph to work on.
d. The **Entity Palette** on the left sidebar contains various targets which can be used & on which transformations can be applied. There are variety of targets such as Domain based, Location based, Person based, etc.
e. To use an entity, click on it, drag and drop it to graph.
f. Provide Entity details, for example, we have selected Domain Entity, in this case, provide target domain name by either click on **Entity Icon or in Property View** in Bottom Right Sidebar.
g. Right click on the Entity to apply Transformations, you can select All, Multiple or Individual Transformations depending upon the requirement. For example, we will use DNS Transformation provided by Paterva.

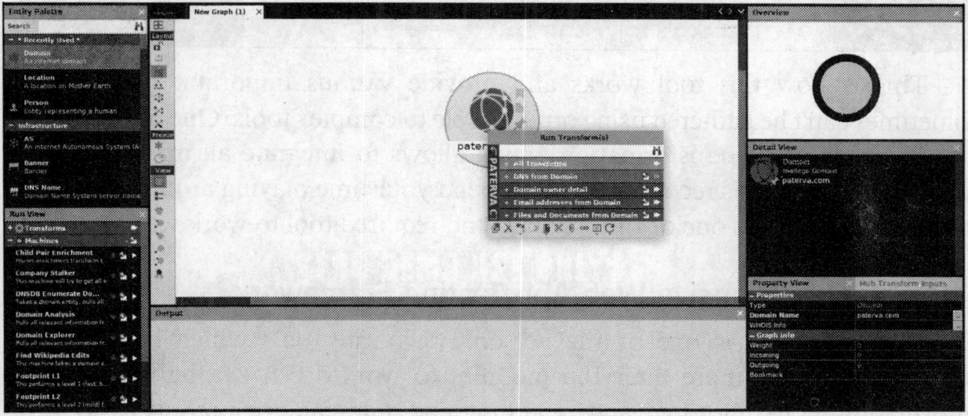

h. Once the transformations will run, it will start showing log details under output section in bottom of graph.
i. After completion of the scan, it will generate a link directed relationship tree with huge dataset of information. Quality of data may vary according to the transformations used. You can click on the particular node to get more details about it. Refer to the below image to know how transformation results will look like in Maltego.

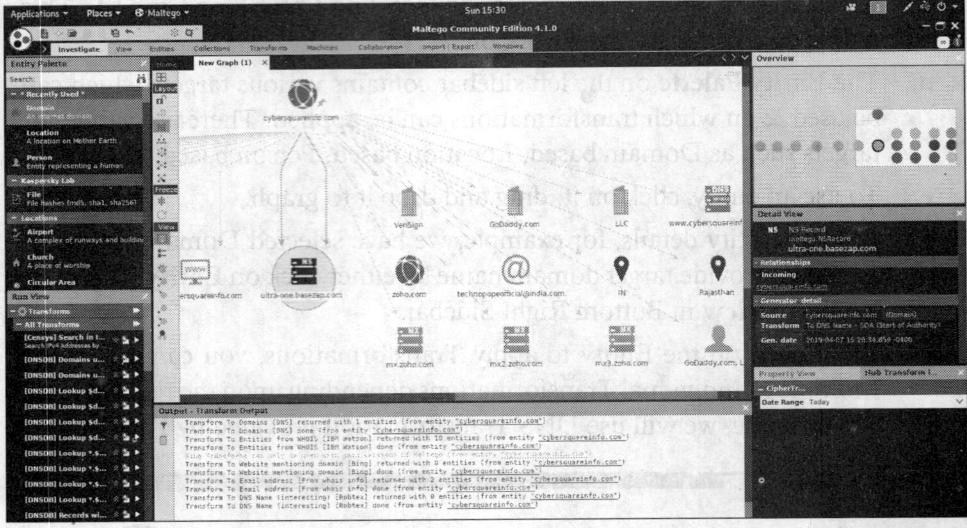

This is how this tool works and provide various important intel which sometimes can't be gathered using other simple to complex tools. One of the major advantages is using transformation which allows to integrate all major services under single tool. It is recommended to spend your time playing around with this tool to master it. It is one of the essential and required tool to work with.

TIDoS – The Offensive Web App Testing Framework

TIDoS Framework is one of my personal favourite tools which has tons of functionalities and more than 100 modules to work on. It can be useful from information gathering to advance scanning and vulnerability analysis as well. It has exploitation modules but is less compared to others and in beta mode. It is expected in the future development of TIDoS framework that it will support a wide range of exploitation modules as well.

TIDoS Framework doesn't come with Kali Linux & you will require to use GitHub to clone its repository & use this tool.

It has 5 Main Phases which are further divided into 14 Sub Phases & 108 modules in total.

Installing TIDoS Framework in Kali Linux

a. Open Terminal & Clone TIDoS repository from GitHub using following command

```
git clone https://github.com/0xInfection/TIDoS-
Framework
```

b. Move to TIDoS directory with following command

```
cd TIDoS-Framework
```

c. Since, there are various modules used in the tool which might not present in your kali Linux environment it is required to install those required packages. There is a requirement file which contains the data for packages required and can be used to install packages using package installer for python PIP.

```
pip install -r requirement.txt
```

d. Provide Execution Permission & Install the tools with the following command

```
chmod +x install
./install
```

e. Now TIDoS Framework is install & ready to work with. You can use tool in the terminal by using following command

```
tidos
```

The initial window of TIDoS framework will look as shown in the below image.

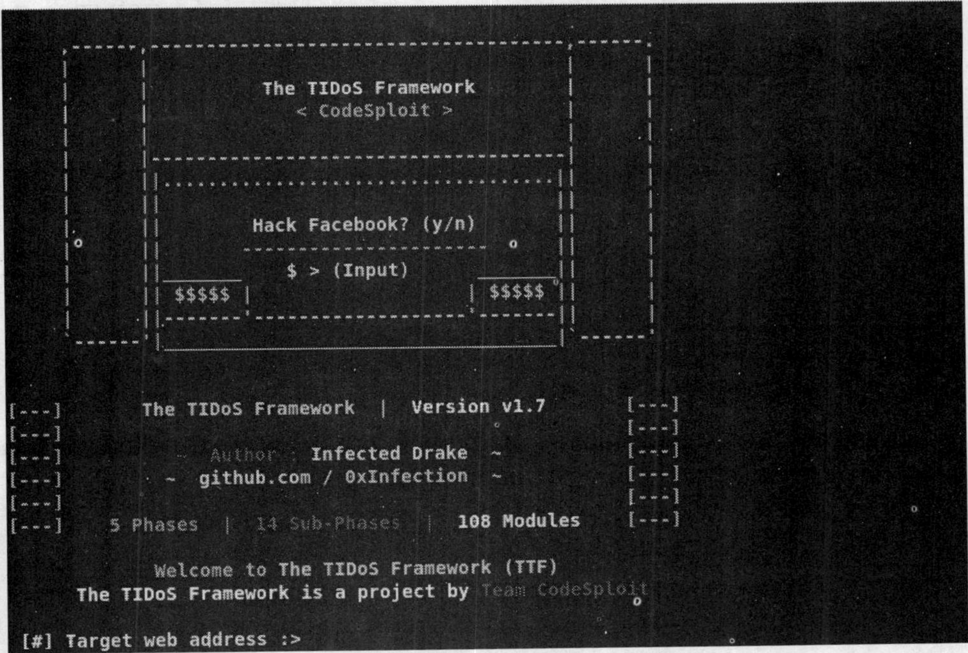

Using TIDoS – Framework

a. Boot Kali Linux & Open Terminal.

b. Start TIDoS Framework with command **tidos**

c. After loading TIDoS Framework it will ask for Target Web Address. Provide the web address of target you want to test.

d. It will ask whether the website uses SSL or Not, Input Y/N, according to your target website.

```
[#] Target web address :> www.cybersquareinfo.com
[#] Does this website use SSL? (y/n) :> y
```

e. It will open further splash screen with following options

Choose from the options below:

```
 [1] Reconnaissance & OSINT (50 modules)
 [2] Scanning & Enumeration (16 modules)
 [3] Vulnerability Analysis (37 modules)
 [4] Exploitation (beta) (1 modules)
 [5] Auxillary Modules (4 modules)
 [99] Say "alvida"! (Exit TIDoS)
 [#] TID :>
<end of Command>
```

f. We will look at Reconnaissance & OSINT Modules for this chapter. In **TID,** input **1** & press enter to get into Reconnaissance & OSINT module.

g. It will ask to choose further modules, we will work on Active Reconnaissance. For this, input **2 in TID** & press Enter.

Choose from the following options:

```
[1] Passive Footprinting (Open Source
Intelligence)
[2] Active Reconnaissance (Gather via Interaction)
[3] Information Disclosure (Errors, Emails, etc)
[99] Back
[#] TID :> 2
<end of command>
```

h. The Active Reconnaissance module have many tools with it, a splash screen will show up with following options to use –

```
[!] Module Selected: Active Reconnaissance
     +----------------+
     |  ACTIVE RECON  |
     +----------------+
     [1] Ping/NPing Enumeration (Adaptative+Debug)
     [2] Grab HTTP Headers (Live Capture)
     [3] Find Allowed HTTP Methods (Via OPTIONS)
     [4] Examine robots.txt and sitemap.xml
     [5] Scrape Comments from Webpage (Regex
Based)
     [6] Perform Advanced Traceroute (TTL Based)
     [7] Find Shared DNS Hosts (NameServer Based)
     [8] Examine SSL Certificate (Absolute)
     [9] CMS Detection (185+ CMSs supported)
```

```
        [10] Apache Status Disclosure (File Based)
        [11] WebDAV HTTP Enumeration (SEARCH,
PROFIND)
        [12] Find PHPInfo File (Regular Bruteforce)
        [13] Enumerate Server behind website
        [14] Alternate Sites (User-Agent Based)
        [15] Common File Bruteforce (5 modules)
        [A] The Auto-Awesome Module
        [99] Back
[#] TID :> A
<end of command>
```

There are 15 different tools like CMS (Content Management System Detection, Web Scrapping, Capturing HTTP Headers (for banner identification), Server Enumeration, etc. This tool allows you to perform all the scans using **The Auto – Awesome Module.** For this example, we will use the same & as shown in above console output, we have chosen option **A in TID.**

The output after performing all the scans will look like below console output:

```
[#] TID :> A
[!] Type Selected : All Modules
[*] Firing up module → Ping Enum
    ============================================
     P I N G / N P I N G   E N U M E R A T I O N
    ============================================
  [!] Pinging website...
  [*] Using adaptative ping and debug mode with
count 5...
  [!] Press Ctrl+C to stop
PING cybersquareinfo.com (23.94.69.34) 56(84)
bytes of data.
[1554463629.425426] 64 bytes from carbon.
allsitecontrol.com (23.94.69.34): icmp_seq=1
ttl=128 time=237 ms
--- cybersquareinfo.com ping statistics ---
5 packets transmitted, 5 received, 0% packet loss,
time 13ms
rtt min/avg/max/mdev =
235.719/243.582/273.103/14.772 ms
[*] Trying NPing (NMap Ping)...
  [~] Result:
Starting Nping 0.7.70 ( https://nmap.org/nping )
at 2019-04-05 11:27 UTC
SENT (0.0034s) ICMP [104.237.144.6 > 23.94.69.34
Echo request (type=8/code=0) id=18487 seq=1] IP
```

```
[ttl=64 id=49152 iplen=28 ]
RCVD (0.2027s) ICMP [23.94.69.34 > 104.237.144.6
Echo reply (type=0/code=0) id=18487 seq=1] IP
[ttl=55 id=47816 iplen=28 ]
SENT (1.0036s) ICMP [104.237.144.6 > 23.94.69.34
Echo request (type=8/code=0) id=18487 seq=3] IP
[ttl=64 id=49152 iplen=28 ]
Max rtt: 199.359ms | Min rtt: 15.575ms | Avg rtt:
74.875ms
Raw packets sent: 4 (112B) | Rcvd: 4 (184B) |
Lost: 0 (0.00%)
Nping done: 1 IP address pinged in 3.06 seconds
  [!] Module Completed → PIng
  [*] Firing up module → Grab Headers
     ==================================
      G R A B   H T T P   H E A D E R S
     ===================================
  [*] Grabbing HTTP Headers...
   Date:  Fri, 05 Apr 2019 11
   Server:  Apache/2.4.39 (cPanel) OpenSSL/1.0.2r
mod_bwlimited/1.4
   X-Pingback:  https
   Link:  <https
   Connection:  close
   Transfer-Encoding:  chunked
   Content-Type:  text/html; charset=UTF-8
  [!] Module Completed → Grabhead
  [*] Firing up module → Robots.txt Hunter
    ==============================
     R O B O T S   C H E C K E R
    ==============================
  [!] Testing for robots.txt...
  [+] Robots.txt found!
  [*] Displaying contents of robots.txt...
User-agent: *
Disallow: /wp-admin/
[+] Sitemap.xml found!
  [*] Displaying contents of sitemap.xml
<?xml version="1.0" encoding="UTF-8"?><?xml-
stylesheet type="text/xsl" href="//
cybersquareinfo.com/core/modules/wordpress-seo/
css/main-sitemap.xsl"?>
<sitemapindex xmlns="http://www.sitemaps.org/
schemas/sitemap/0.9">
```

```
. . .
. . .
</sitemapindex>
  [!] Module Completed → Robot Hunter
  [*] Firing up module → Comments Scraper
      ================================
      C O M M E N T S   S C R A P E R
      ================================
  [It is recommended to run ScanEnum/Crawlers
        before running this module]
  [*] Importing links...
  [*] Making the request...
. . .
. . .
. . .
<Rest of Command Output in similar manner>
<End of command>
```

This is how TIDoS works to calculate various intel by allowing you to choose run multiple tools at once. There are other Reconnaissance & OSINT modules in this tool which can be self-explored easily. We have almost used every methodology tools and techniques present in this tool throughout the book but this can be considered as a collaborative tool for the whole process.

Summary

In this chapter, we have worked on many tools used by Security Researchers & Professionals for information gathering and reconnaissance. These tools are fairly and widely popular among information security community, and some tools are adapted by top level organizations and companies as well. This is highly recommended and suggested to practice all the tool to get more consistency and better understanding while working with them.

We have already seen many tools, now in the further chapter, we will look at network scanning where we will discover about various services, some tools & how things work on the network in the backend. It will cover portions of service scanning, packet capturing, traffic analysis and further methodologies used for advanced scanning.

9 Network Service Scanning & Advance Scanning Techniques

Module Outlines

- Introduction to Scanning
- Nmap – The Network Mapper
- Nmap First Look
- Basics of Port Scanning using Nmap
- Service & Version Scanning using Nmap
- OS Detection using Nmap
- Nmap Scripting Engine
- Hping – Active Network Security Tool
- Banner Grabbing & its Tools
- Proxy Servers & Proxy Chaining
- TOR – The Anonymity Browser

Scanning is yet another important phase in penetration testing or investigating a digital target. It involves interaction with the target either actively or passively to gather intel such network services, ports, protocols, OS & other relevant information about the target system. Unlike, Information Gathering where we have looked at various basic information such as IP Address, Network status, etc. In this chapter, we will crawl the target system further to get in-depth knowledge about it. It will provide us with information which will help us for vulnerability assessment & exploitation.

This is the final phase where all the findings & target system's auditing take place, after this, we plan for vulnerability assessment on the basis of the information gathering until now & perform exploitation.

In most of the cases, Scanning provides us with much relevant and useful information which can directly be used for exploiting the target or we can say that Scanning sometimes also involves vulnerability assessment as well. It is important to learn & practice scanning methodologies before trying to exploit or investigate the target directly because in many cases we have to be careful about our approaches else we may end up in committing an unintentional Cyber Crime which can lend us into big trouble. *Also, for learning purpose don't try the tools and methodologies on any web application or target system because sometimes generating huge traffic on the target through your system again and again may cause a small level Denial of Service attack on very small-scale targets.*

In the networking chapter, we have already discussed various ports like FTP, SNMP, HTTPS, HTTP, etc. and protocols like TCP & UDP. We learned concepts of how connection is established using three-way handshake and how four-way handshake works. Further, in this chapter, we will look at scanning various services and flag-based scanning, banner grabbing and how proxies work. We will mainly look at one of the widely used and most popular tools **Nmap** (network mapper).

Nmap – The Network Mapper

Nmap is one of the widely used and most popular tools among cyber security professionals, security researchers, hackers & network engineers and learners as well. It is an open source licensed tool mainly used for performing discover such as open ports, operating systems, etc. and auditing or determining security over the network.

Nmap is a command line utility which comes pre-installed with Kali Linux. You can also download it for other operating systems from https://nmap.org/download.html

Nmap also has an official graphical user interface version known as **Zenmap.** For this chapter & book, we will look at the command line version *i.e.* Nmap. Zenmap can also be used similarly.

Nmap has a scripting engine known as **Nmap Scripting Engine – NSE** which is a powerful extension for Nmap which allows various scripts to connect with Nmap & extend its scope and potential to next level.

Nmap has several other components such as a flexible data transfer, redirection, and debugging tool (Ncat), a utility for comparing scan results (Ndiff), and a packet generation and response analysis tool (Nping). (source – nmap.org)

Nmap was named "Security Product of the Year" by Linux Journal, Info World, LinuxQuestions.Org, and Codetalker Digest. It was even featured in twelve movies, including The Matrix Reloaded, Die Hard 4, Girl with the Dragon Tattoo, and The Bourne Ultimatum. (source – nmap.org)

Why Nmap is a preferred choice

(source – nmap.org)

Flexible: Supports dozens of advanced techniques for mapping out networks filled with IP filters, firewalls, routers, and other obstacles. This includes many port scanning mechanisms (both TCP & UDP), OS detection, version detection, ping sweeps, and more. See the documentation page.

Powerful: Nmap has been used to scan huge networks of literally hundreds of thousands of machines.

Portable: Most operating systems are supported, including Linux, Microsoft Windows, FreeBSD, OpenBSD, Solaris, IRIX, Mac OS X, HP-UX, NetBSD, Sun OS, Amiga, and more.

Easy: While Nmap offers a rich set of advanced features for power users, you can start out as simply as "nmap -v -A targethost". Both traditional command line and graphical (GUI) versions are available to suit your preference. Binaries are available for those who do not wish to compile Nmap from source.

Free: The primary goals of the Nmap Project is to help make the Internet a little more secure and to provide administrators/auditors/hackers with an advanced tool for exploring their networks. Nmap is available for free download, and also comes with full source code that you may modify and redistribute under the terms of the license.

Well Documented: Significant effort has been put into comprehensive and up-to-date man pages, whitepapers, tutorials, and even a whole book! Find them in multiple languages here.

Supported: While Nmap comes with no warranty, it is well supported by a vibrant community of developers and users. Most of this interaction occurs on the Nmap mailing lists. Most bug reports and questions should be sent to the nmap-dev list, but only after you read the guidelines. We recommend that all users subscribe to the low-traffic nmap-hackers announcement list. You can also find Nmap on Facebook and Twitter. For real-time chat, join the #nmap channel on Freenode or EFNet.

Acclaimed: Nmap has won numerous awards, including "Information Security Product of the Year" by Linux Journal, Info World and Codetalker Digest. It has been featured in hundreds of magazine articles, several movies, dozens of books, and one comic book series. Visit the press page for further details.

Popular: Thousands of people download Nmap every day, and it is included with many operating systems (Redhat Linux, Debian Linux, Gentoo, FreeBSD, OpenBSD, etc). It is among the top ten (out of 30,000) programs at the Freshmeat. Net repository. This is important because it lends Nmap its vibrant development and user support communities.

Nmap First Look

a. Boot Kali Linux & Start the Terminal

b. Type the following command to start Nmap –

```
> nmap
```

c. When you start nmap with no additional parameter, it will display the options screen like shown below:

   (for a complete list of options)

```
root@kali:~# nmap
Nmap 7.70 ( https://nmap.org )
Usage: nmap [Scan Type(s)] [Options] {target
specification}
TARGET SPECIFICATION:
  Can pass hostnames, IP addresses, networks, etc.
  Ex: scanme.nmap.org, microsoft.com/24,
192.168.0.1; 10.0.0-255.1-254
  -iL <inputfilename>: Input from list of hosts/
networks
  -iR <num hosts>: Choose random targets
  --exclude <host1[,host2][,host3],...>: Exclude
hosts/networks
SCAN TECHNIQUES:
  -sS/sT/sA/sW/sM: TCP SYN/Connect()/ACK/Window/
Maimon scans
  -sU: UDP Scan
  -sN/sF/sX: TCP Null, FIN, and Xmas scans
  --scanflags <flags>: Customize TCP scan flags
  -sI <zombie host[:probeport]>: Idle scan
PORT SPECIFICATION AND SCAN ORDER:
  -p <port ranges>: Only scan specified ports
    Ex: -p22; -p1-65535; -p U:53,111,137,T:21-
25,80,139,8080,S:9
  --exclude-ports <port ranges>: Exclude the
specified ports from scanning
SERVICE/VERSION DETECTION:
  -sV: Probe open ports to determine service/
version info
  --version-intensity <level>: Set from 0 (light)
to 9 (try all probes)
SCRIPT SCAN:
  -sC: equivalent to --script=default
  --script=<Lua scripts>: <Lua scripts> is a comma
separated list of
           directories, script-files or script-
categories
OS DETECTION:
  -O: Enable OS detection
  --osscan-limit: Limit OS detection to promising
targets
  --osscan-guess: Guess OS more aggressively
```

```
TIMING AND PERFORMANCE:
  Options which take <time> are in seconds, or append 'ms' (milliseconds),
  's' (seconds), 'm' (minutes), or 'h' (hours) to the value (e.g. 30m).
  -T<0-5>: Set timing template (higher is faster)
FIREWALL/IDS EVASION AND SPOOFING:
  -f; --mtu <val>: fragment packets (optionally w/ given MTU)
  -D <decoy1,decoy2[,ME],...>: Cloak a scan with decoys
  -S <IP_Address>: Spoof source address
MISC:
  -6: Enable IPv6 scanning
  -A: Enable OS detection, version detection, script scanning, and traceroute
  -V: Print version number
  -h: Print this help summary page.
EXAMPLES:
  nmap -v -A scanme.nmap.org
  nmap -v -sn 192.168.0.0/16 10.0.0.0/8
  nmap -v -iR 10000 -Pn -p 80
SEE THE MAN PAGE (https://nmap.org/book/man.html)
FOR MORE OPTIONS AND EXAMPLES
<end of command>
```

d. There are lots of options in nmap and detailed list can be seen on Manual page (reference link is shown in above output).

e. The general syntax for using nmap as shown in above output is –

```
> nmap [Scan Type(s)] [Options] {target specification}
```

f. For example, we will take an illustration of how nmap works with a simple example as shown in above output

```
> nmap -v -A scanme.nmap.org
```

g. Output for above example will look like following –

```
root@kali:~# nmap -v -A scanme.nmap.org
Starting Nmap 7.70 ( https://nmap.org )
NSE: Loaded 148 scripts for scanning.
NSE: Script Pre-scanning.
Initiating NSE at 06:59
Completed NSE at 06:59, 0.00s elapsed
```

```
Initiating NSE at 06:59
Completed NSE at 06:59, 0.00s elapsed
Initiating Ping Scan at 06:59
Scanning scanme.nmap.org (45.33.32.156) [1000
ports]
Discovered open port 22/tcp on 45.33.32.156
Discovered open port 80/tcp on 45.33.32.156
Increasing send delay for 45.33.32.156 from 0 to
5 due to 11 out of 16 dropped probes since last
increase.
adjust_timeouts2: packet supposedly had rtt of
8336069 microseconds.  Ignoring time.
Increasing send delay for 45.33.32.156 from 40 to
80 due to 16 out of 52 dropped probes since last
increase.
SYN Stealth Scan Timing: About 43.55% done; ETC:
07:19 (0:11:19 remaining)
Discovered open port 31337/tcp on 45.33.32.156
SYN Stealth Scan Timing: About 46.33% done; ETC:
07:24 (0:13:26 remaining)
<end of command>
```

Basics of Port Scanning

Nmap is one of the efficient port scanners and by default scan first 1000 tcp ports on the target *i.e.* when you use **nmap <target>** command directly without specifying any port or port range, it will scan first 1000 tcp ports.

Nmap provides ports into six states, which are –

(source - https://nmap.org/book/man-port-scanning-basics.html)

Open

An application is actively accepting TCP connections, UDP datagrams or SCTP associations on this port. Finding these is often the primary goal of port scanning. Security-minded people know that each open port is an avenue for attack.

Closed

A closed port is accessible (it receives and responds to Nmap probe packets), but there is no application listening on it. They can be helpful in showing that a host is up on an IP address (host discovery, or ping scanning), and as part of OS detection.

Filtered

Nmap cannot determine whether the port is open because packet filtering prevents its probes from reaching the port. The filtering could be from a dedicated firewall device, router rules, or host-based firewall software.

Unfiltered

The unfiltered state means that a port is accessible, but Nmap is unable to determine whether it is open or closed. Only the ACK scan, which is used to map firewall rulesets, classifies ports into this state.

Open | Filtered

Nmap places ports in this state when it is unable to determine whether a port is open or filtered. This occurs for scan types in which open ports give no response. The lack of response could also mean that a packet filter dropped the probe or any response it elicited.

Closed | Filtered

This state is used when Nmap is unable to determine whether a port is closed or filtered. It is only used for the IP ID idle scan.

Various Port & Flag Based Scanning with Nmap

Important Points

a. To specify port range use following optional parameter

```
> -p <port range>
Ex: nmap -sS -p 0-100 scanme.nmap.org
```

b. To select all ports use following optional parameter

```
> -p-
Ex: nmap -sS -p- scanme.nmap.org
```

c. To perform a fast scan with limited ports use following optional parameter

```
> -F
Ex: nmap -sS -F scanme.nmap.org
d. To see the backend processing information use
following optional parameter -
> -v
Ex: nmap -v -sS scanme.nmap.org
```

1. TCP SYN Scan

TCP SYN Scan is also referred as **Half-Open Scan.** It is quick, default & most popular scan and has ability to scan thousands of ports within seconds (considering fair internet connection not restricted by firewalls). It never complete whole 3-way handshake and provides clear results between open, closed and filtered ports.

Flag for SYN Scan: `-sS`

Syntax: `nmap -sS <target> <other optional parameters>`

Performing TCP SYN Scan

a. Boot Kali Linux & Open Terminal.

b. Use following command for TCP SYN Scan & check below output

```
root@kali:~# nmap -sS scanme.nmap.org
Starting Nmap 7.70 ( https://nmap.org )
RTTVAR has grown to over 2.3 seconds, decreasing
to 2.0
RTTVAR has grown to over 2.3 seconds, decreasing
to 2.0
Nmap scan report for scanme.nmap.org
(45.33.32.156)
Host is up (2.4s latency).
Other addresses for scanme.nmap.org (not scanned):
2600:3c01::f03c:91ff:fe18:bb2f
Not shown: 989 closed ports
PORT        STATE      SERVICE
22/tcp      open       ssh
25/tcp      filtered   smtp
80/tcp      open       http
135/tcp     filtered   msrpc
139/tcp     filtered   netbios-ssn
445/tcp     filtered   microsoft-ds
514/tcp     filtered   shell
2049/tcp    filtered   nfs
Nmap done: 1 IP address (1 host up) scanned in
336.13 seconds
<end of command>
```

2. *TCP Connect Scan*

TCP Connect scan detects open ports by completing the 3-way handshake process (establishes the full connection) and break down connecting by sending RST packet to the target. If SYN Scan is not used, this is the default scan and doesn't require any superuser privileges.

In this scan, we send a syn packet to target on specified porn numbers, depending upon port's state, the following can happen –

a. If the port is open, we receive an SYN + ACK packet back along with the required data. After this we send ACK packet and kill connection by sending RST Packet.

b. If the port is closed, we receive an RST packet in response.

Flag for SYN Scan: `-sT`

Syntax: `nmap -sT <target> <other optional parameters>`

Performing TCP SYN Scan –

a. Boot Kali Linux & Open Terminal.

b. Use the following command for TCP Connect Scan & check below output

```
root@kali:~# nmap -sT  scanme.nmap.org -p 0-100
Starting Nmap 7.70 ( https://nmap.org )
Nmap scan report for scanme.nmap.org
(45.33.32.156)
Host is up (0.31s latency).
Other addresses for scanme.nmap.org (not scanned):
2600:3c01::f03c:91ff:fe18:bb2f
Not shown: 99 filtered ports
PORT       STATE           SERVICE
22/tcp     open            ssh
80/tcp     open            http
Nmap done: 1 IP address (1 host up) scanned in
22.13 seconds
<end of command>
```

3. *UDP Scan*

There are some services and protocols which operates on UDP such as DNS & DHCP. UDP Scan works by sending UDP Packets to every specified port on the target system. It can work in combination with TCP Scans such as SYN Scan to check both protocols in the same scan.

It is usually slower and complex compared to TCP Scans due to which it is usually ignored by pentesters.

Flag for UDP Scan: `-sU`

Syntax: `nmap -sU <target> <other optional parameters>`

Performing UDP Scan

a. Boot Kali Linux & Open Terminal.

b. Use the following command for UDP Scan & check the below output –

```
root@kali:~# nmap -sU scanme.nmap.org
Starting Nmap 7.70 ( https://nmap.org )
Nmap scan report for scanme.nmap.org
(45.33.32.156)
Host is up (0.00034s latency).
Other addresses for scanme.nmap.org (not scanned):
2600:3c01::f03c:91ff:fe18:bb2f
All 1000 scanned ports on scanme.nmap.org
(45.33.32.156) are open|filtered
Nmap done: 1 IP address (1 host up) scanned in
7.59 seconds
<end of command>
```

4. *SCTP INIT Scan*

SCTP is a relatively new alternative to the TCP and UDP protocols, combining

most characteristics of both and also adding new features like multi-homing and multi-streaming. It is mostly being used for **SS7/SIGTRAN** related services but has the potential to be used for other applications as well. SCTP INIT scan is the SCTP equivalent of a TCP SYN scan. It can be performed quickly, scanning thousands of ports per second on a fast network not hampered by restrictive firewalls. Like SYN scan, INIT scan is relatively unobtrusive and stealthy, since it never completes SCTP associations. It also allows clear, reliable differentiation between the open, closed, and filtered states.
(source – nmap.org)

Flag for SCTP INIT Scan: `-sY`

Syntax: `nmap -sY <target> <other optional parameters>`

Performing SCTP INIT Scan

a. Boot Kali Linux & Open Terminal.
b. Use the following command for SCTP INIT Scan & check below output–

```
root@kali:~# nmap -sY scanme.nmap.org
Starting Nmap 7.70 ( https://nmap.org )
Nmap scan report for scanme.nmap.org
(45.33.32.156)
Host is up (0.000053s latency).
Other addresses for scanme.nmap.org (not scanned):
2600:3c01::f03c:91ff:fe18:bb2f
All 52 scanned ports on scanme.nmap.org
(45.33.32.156) are filtered
Nmap done: 1 IP address (1 host up) scanned in
4.62 seconds
<end of command>
```

5. *XMAS SCAN*

Xmas scan is a type of scan which exploits a loophole present in TCP RFC to put a fine line between open and closed ports. It will not work against any latest version of windows operating system and will work for OSes having TCP's RFC-793 implementation. In this scan, we send a TCP Frame to a remote device with FIN, Push & URG flag set. Along with XMAS Scan, we will also look at Null & Fin Scan which works by it.

In NULL Scan, TCP flag header is set to 0.

In FIN Scan, Only FIN bit is set in TCP flag header.

In Xmas Scan, FIN, PSH & URG bits are set in TCP flag header.

Flag for Null Scan: `-sN`

Flag for Fin Scan: `-sF`

Flag for Xmas Scan: `-sX`

Syntax: `nmap -sX/N/F <target> <other optional parameters>`

Performing Xmas Scan

a. Boot Kali Linux & Open Terminal.

b. Use following command for Xmas Scan & check below output –

```
root@kali:~# nmap -v -sX scanme.nmap.org -p 0-500
Starting Nmap 7.70 ( https://nmap.org )
Initiating Ping Scan at 09:27
Scanning scanme.nmap.org (45.33.32.156) [4 ports]
Completed Ping Scan at 09:27, 0.03s elapsed (1
total hosts)
Initiating Parallel DNS resolution of 1 host. at
09:27
Completed Parallel DNS resolution of 1 host. at
09:27, 0.46s elapsed
Initiating XMAS Scan at 09:27
Scanning scanme.nmap.org (45.33.32.156) [501
ports]
Completed XMAS Scan at 09:27, 3.19s elapsed (501
total ports)
Nmap scan report for scanme.nmap.org
(45.33.32.156)
Host is up (0.00048s latency).
Other addresses for scanme.nmap.org (not scanned):
2600:3c01::f03c:91ff:fe18:bb2f
All 501 scanned ports on scanme.nmap.org
(45.33.32.156) are open|filtered
Read data files from: /usr/bin/../share/nmap
Nmap done: 1 IP address (1 host up) scanned in
4.30 seconds
           Raw packets sent: 1008 (40.312KB) |
Rcvd: 4 (160B)
<end of command>
```

6. *TCP Maimon Scan*

The Maimon scan is named after its discoverer, Uriel Maimon. He described the technique in Phrack Magazine issue #49 (November 1996). Nmap, which included this technique, was released two issues later. This technique is the same as NULL, FIN, and Xmas scans, except that the probe is FIN/ACK. According to RFC 793 (TCP), a RST packet should be generated in response to such a probe whether the port is open or closed. However, Uriel noticed that many BSD-derived systems simply drop the packet if the port is open.

(source – nmap.org)

Flag for Xmas Scan: `-sM`

Syntax: `nmap -sM <target> <other optional parameters>`

It can be performed similar as per the above scans.

7. *TCP Custom Flag Scan*

This functionality of nmap allows you to design a TCP scan by specifying TCP Flags according to your requirement.

— **scanflags** argument is used to specify Custom TCP Scan.

To use this scan, just combine the symbolic/numeric identifiers of each flag and perform the scan.

Syntax: `nmap --scanflags <flag_combination> <target> <other optional parameters>`

Ex: `nmap --scanflags SYNURGFIN scanme.nmap.org`

This will choose scan based on SYN, URG & FIN Flags. This scan can be performed similarly as per the above scans.

Version & Service Detection with Nmap

Nmap is most popular among other port scanners, it has pre-built functionality which allows you to detect the services running on specific ports & their versions. It can be carried out using Version & Service Scan option in Nmap which an optional parameter.

Flag for Service & Version Scan: `-sV`

Syntax: `nmap -sV <target> <other optional parameters>`

Performing Service & Version Scan

a. Boot Kali Linux & Open Terminal.

b. Use the following command for Service & Version Scan & check below output

```
root@kali:~# nmap  -sSV scanme.nmap.org
Starting Nmap 7.70 ( https://nmap.org )
Warning: 45.33.32.156 giving up on port because
retransmission cap hit (10).
Nmap scan report for scanme.nmap.org
(45.33.32.156)
Host is up (0.28s latency).
Other addresses for scanme.nmap.org (not scanned):
2600:3c01::f03c:91ff:fe18:bb2f
Not shown: 992 closed ports
PORT         STATE        SERVICE       VERSION
22/tcp       open         ssh           OpenSSH 6.6.1p1
25/tcp       filtered     smtp
80/tcp       open         http         Apache httpd
2.4.7
135/tcp      filtered     msrpc
```

```
139/tcp    filtered    netbios-ssn
Service Info: OS: Linux; CPE: cpe:/o:linux:linux_
kernel
Service detection performed. Please report any
incorrect results at https://nmap.org/submit/ .
Nmap done: 1 IP address (1 host up) scanned in
98.04 seconds
<end of command>
```

OS Detection with Nmap

Operating System detection is one of the best features of Nmap, which allows us to detect the target's OS by looking into TCP/IP stack implemented on the target. Each Operating System varies in TCP/IP Stack implementations which allows us to gather the information about the operating system just by crawling into stack implementation and looking for differences.

Flag for OS Detection: `-sO`

Flag for Guessing OS Detection: `--osscan-guess; --fuzzy`

Syntax: `nmap -sO <target> <other optional parameters>`

Performing OS Detection

a. Boot Kali Linux & Open Terminal.

b. Use the following command for OS Detection & check below output –

```
root@kali:~# nmap -O -v scanme.nmap.org
Starting Nmap 7.70 ( https://nmap.org )
Initiating Ping Scan at 11:04
Scanning scanme.nmap.org (45.33.32.156) [4 ports]
Completed Ping Scan at 11:04, 0.04s elapsed (1
total hosts)
Initiating SYN Stealth Scan at 11:04
Initiating OS detection (try #1) against scanme.
nmap.org (45.33.32.156)
Retrying OS detection (try #2) against scanme.
nmap.org (45.33.32.156)
Nmap scan report for scanme.nmap.org
(45.33.32.156)
Host is up (0.42s latency).
Other addresses for scanme.nmap.org (not scanned):
2600:3c01::f03c:91ff:fe18:bb2f
Not shown: 990 closed ports
PORT      STATE    SERVICE
22/tcp    open     ssh
25/tcp    filtered smtp
80/tcp    open     http
```

```
135/tcp   filtered msrpc
139/tcp   filtered netbios-ssn
445/tcp   filtered microsoft-ds
514/tcp   filtered shell
Aggressive OS guesses: Actiontec MI424WR-GEN3I WAP
(96%), DD-WRT v24-sp2 (Linux 2.4.37) (94%), Linux
3.2 (94%), Linux 4.4 (94%), Microsoft Windows XP
SP3 or Windows 7 or Windows Server 2012 (93%),
Microsoft Windows XP SP3 (93%), BlueArc Titan 2100
NAS device (88%)
No exact OS matches for host (test conditions non-
ideal).
TCP Sequence Prediction: Difficulty=252 (Good
luck!)
IP ID Sequence Generation: Incremental
Nmap done: 1 IP address (1 host up) scanned in
187.23 seconds
<end of command>
```

c. In the above example, the nmap fails to exactly determine the operating system so it runs **Aggressive OS Guesses** and you can see the results based with accuracy in percentage in the above output.

Nmap Scripting Engine (NSE)

Nmap Scripting Engine (NSE) is one of the most powerful and advanced features of Nmap. It allows us to write simple scripts or use existing scripts for specified jobs using nmap.

These scripts are written in the **LUA Programming Language.**

According to nmap.org, NSE is designed with following in mind *(source – nmap.org)*

Network Discovery

This is Nmap's bread and butter. Examples include looking up whois data based on the target domain, querying ARIN, RIPE, or APNIC for the target IP to determine ownership, performing identd lookups on open ports, SNMP queries, and listing available NFS/SMB/RPC shares and services.

More Sophisticated Version Detection

The Nmap version detection system is able to recognize thousands of different services through its probe and regular expression signature based matching system, but it cannot recognize everything.

Vulnerability Detection

When a new vulnerability is discovered, you often want to scan your networks quickly to identify vulnerable systems before the bad guys do. While Nmap isn't a comprehensive vulnerability scanner, NSE is powerful enough to handle even demanding vulnerability checks. When the Heartbleed bug affected hundreds of thousands of systems worldwide, Nmap's developers responded with the ssl-heartbleed detection script within 2 days.

Backdoor Detection

Many attackers and some automated worms leave backdoors to enable later re-entry. Some of these can be detected by Nmap's regular expression-based version detection, but more complex worms and backdoors require NSE's advanced capabilities to reliably detect.

Vulnerability Exploitation

As a general scripting language, NSE can even be used to exploit vulnerabilities rather than just find them. The capability to add custom exploit scripts may be valuable for some people (particularly penetration testers), though we aren't planning to turn Nmap into an exploitation framework such as Metasploit.

Flag for NSE: `-sC; --script (for custom scripts)`

Syntax: `nmap -sC <target> <other optional parameters>`

Or

nmap –script <script> <target> <optional parameters>

Using Nmap Scripting Engine

a. Boot Kali Linux & Start Terminal

b. Refer to the below example & Sample output for working of NSE –

```
root@kali:~# nmap -sC -p21,25,80 -T4 scanme.nmap.
org
Starting Nmap 7.70 ( https://nmap.org )
Nmap scan report for scanme.nmap.org
(45.33.32.156)
Host is up (0.037s latency).
Other addresses for scanme.nmap.org (not scanned):
2600:3c01::f03c:91ff:fe18:bb2f
PORT        STATE       SERVICE
21/tcp      filtered    ftp
25/tcp      filtered    smtp
80/tcp      open        http
|_http-title: Go ahead and ScanMe!
Nmap done: 1 IP address (1 host up) scanned in
9.31 seconds
<end of command>
```

Hping – Active Network Security Tool

Hping is a powerful command line-based TCP/IP packet assembler/analyser utility.

According to hping.org, While hping was mainly used as a security tool in the past, it can be used in many ways by people that don't care about security to test networks and hosts. A subset of the stuff you can do using hping:

- Firewall testing
- Advanced port scanning
- Network testing, using different protocols, TOS, fragmentation
- Manual path MTU discovery
- Advanced traceroute, under all the supported protocols
- Remote OS fingerprinting
- Remote uptime guessing
- TCP/IP stacks auditing
- hping can also be useful to students that are learning TCP/IP.

Hping3 is the latest version of hping utility, and it comes pre-built with Kali Linux.

To check various options available with hping3, open kali linux terminal and use the following command –

```
> man hping3

BASE OPTIONS
-c, --count <count>: Stop after sending (and
receiving) count response packets.
-i, -interval: Wait the specified number of
seconds or micro seconds between sending each
packet.
--fast: Alias for -i u10000. Hping will send 10
packets for second.
--flood: Sent packets as fast as possible, without
taking care to show incoming replies.
-I, --interface <interface name>: By default, on
Linux and BSD systems hping3 uses default routing
interface.
-V, --verbose: Enable verbose output.
```

The above output displays important base options from the hping3 manual. It is recommended to read the hping3 manual to learn about various options such as selecting protocols, IP related options, etc. to get a better understanding of the tool. In this chapter, we will look at a simple hping3 scan to know how it works in practical scenarios.

Using hping3 for simple SYN Flood

c. Boot Kali Linux & Start Terminal

d. Refer to below example & Sample output for working of simple SYN Flood using hping3

```
root@kali:~# hping3 -S --flood -V scanme.nmap.org
using eth0, addr: 192.168.121.137, MTU: 1500
HPING scanme.nmap.org (eth0 45.33.32.156): S set,
40 headers + 0 data bytes
hping in flood mode, no replies will be shown
^C
--- scanme.nmap.org hping statistic ---
63648 packets transmitted, 0 packets received,
100% packet loss
round-trip min/avg/max = 0.0/0.0/0.0 ms
<end of command>
```

Performing Smurf Attack using hping3

Smurf Attack is a type of Denial of Service (DoS) attack which floods the target by using spoofed broadcast ping messages.

a. Boot Kali Linux & Start Terminal.

b. Refer to below example & Sample output for working of Smurf Attack using hping3

```
root@kali:~# hping3 -1 --flood -a scanme.nmap.org
10.0.2.12
HPING 10.0.2.12 (eth0 10.0.2.12): icmp mode set,
28 headers + 0 data bytes
hping in flood mode, no replies will be shown
^C
--- 10.0.2.12 hping statistic ---
112265 packets transmitted, 0 packets received,
100% packet loss
round-trip min/avg/max = 0.0/0.0/0.0 ms
<end of command>
```

Banner Grabbing

The banner is nothing but a text message that is returned from the host when a request is made. It contains information about the header, version, about a service or sometimes can provide sensitive information as well.

Banner Grabbing refers to a process of capturing banners or collecting details about any remote systems on a network & services running on its open ports.

Banner Grabbing is also referred as Operating System Fingerprinting.

Telnet is one of the popular protocols over which banner grabbing can be performed. A general banner grabbing request using telnet service looks like following –

```
telnet hostname 80
For Ex: telnet www.cybersquareinfo.com 80
```

If the request is successful, the server returns a HTML banner which contains various information about it.

Banner Grabbing is usually divided into two categories :

1. Active Banner Grabbing

In active banner grabbing, we send some specially crafted packets to remote system & then wait to responses and after receiving we observe them. These responses are further compared with various databases which contain information about the operating system to find out the target operating system.

We are able to find out the Operating System because as we already discussed different operating system have different TCP/IP Stack Implementations.

2. Passive Banner Grabbing

Passive banner grabbing involves collecting banners or header information without directly interacting with the target system. It involves various ways such as **Banner Grabbing from Error Messages, Capturing Packets over the network, Information retrieved from Extensions (such as .php, .aspx)**, etc.

Banner grabbing can be done using various tools, In this chapter, we will look at some important tools used for banner grabbing.

Banner Grabbing with Nmap

Syntax – `nmap -sV -script=banner <target>`

a. Boot Kali Linux & Start Terminal

b. Refer to below example & Sample output for working of Banner Grabbing using Nmap

```
root@kali:~# nmap -sV --script=banner -p 0-100
scanme.nmap.org
Starting Nmap 7.70 ( https://nmap.org )
Nmap scan report for scanme.nmap.org
(45.33.32.156)
Host is up (0.056s latency).
Other addresses for scanme.nmap.org (not scanned):
2600:3c01::f03c:91ff:fe18:bb2f
Not shown: 98 filtered ports
PORT      STATE     SERVICE   VERSION
22/tcp    open      ssh            OpenSSH
6.6.1p1 Ubuntu
```

```
|_banner: SSH-2.0-OpenSSH_6.6.1p1 Ubuntu-
2ubuntu2.11
23/tcp    closed    telnet
80/tcp    open      http        Apache httpd
2.4.7 ((Ubuntu))
|_http-server-header: Apache/2.4.7 (Ubuntu)
Service Info: OS: Linux; CPE: cpe:/o:linux:linux_
kernel
Nmap done: 1 IP address (1 host up) scanned in
27.04 seconds
<end of command>
```

Banner Grabbing with cURL

Syntax – `curl -s -I <target>`

a. Boot Kali Linux & Start Terminal
b. Refer to below example & Sample output for working of Banner Grabbing using cURL –

```
root@kali:~# curl -s -I scanme.nmap.org | grep -e
"Server:"
Server: Apache/2.4.7 (Ubuntu)
<end of command>
```

The grep command will search for specific keyword provided under " ". In above example, it directly outputs Server line only.

Banner Grabbing with Netcat

Syntax – `nc -v <target> <port>`

a. Boot Kali Linux & Start Terminal
b. Refer to below example & Sample output for working of Banner Grabbing using Netcat –

```
root@kali:~# nc -v scanme.nmap.org 80
scanme.nmap.org [45.33.32.156] 80 (http) open
GET /HTTP/ 1.0
HTTP/1.1 400 Bad Request
Date: Sun, 07 Apr 2019 18:12:57 GMT
Server: Apache/2.4.7 (Ubuntu)
Content-Length: 306
Connection: close
Content-Type: text/html; charset=iso-8859-1
<!DOCTYPE HTML PUBLIC "-//IETF//DTD HTML 2.0//EN">
<html><head>
<title>400 Bad Request</title>
</head><body>
<h1>Bad Request</h1>
```

```
<p>Your browser sent a request that this server
could not understand. <br />
</p>
<hr>
<address>Apache/2.4.7 (Ubuntu) Server at scanme.
nmap.org Port 80</address>
</body></html>
<end of command>
```

In above example, after entering into Netcat, we have to provide request header according to the port used. In this case, for http (port 80), we used **GET / HTTP/1.0**

Banner Grabbing with DMitry

Syntax – `dmitry -b <target>`

a. Boot Kali Linux & Start Terminal

b. Refer to below example & Sample output for working of Banner Grabbing using DMitry –

```
root@kali:~# dmitry -b 45.33.32.156
Deepmagic Information Gathering Tool
"There be some deep magic going on"
HostIP:45.33.32.156
HostName:scanme.nmap.org
Gathered TCP Port information for 45.33.32.156
-------------------------------
 Port           State
22/tcp          open
>> SSH-2.0-OpenSSH_6.6.1p1 Ubuntu-2ubuntu2.11
80/tcp          open
Portscan Finished: Scanned 150 ports, 69 ports
were in state closed
All scans completed, exiting
<end of command>
```

Proxy Servers

A Proxy server is an application that can serve as an intermediary for connecting with other computers. In general scenarios, when you connect to any network, your own IP address is used for connection establishment. By using proxy servers, you can map your identity behind a chain of other ip addresses and appear to be someone else while connecting to the network. This leads to anonymity over the internet but doesn't mean that your identity is not traceable.

Why are Proxy Servers used?

a. A Proxy server is used to hide source IP address to keep identity hidden over the internet.

b. It is used to mask actual source to attack by impersonating fake source by use of a proxy.

c. It can be used to remotely access Intranets or other websites which are normally off limits.

d. To Interrupt all the requests sent by a legit user and transmit them to a third destination. Hence victims will only be able to identity a proxy server and fall prey.

e. Attackers can use multiple chain proxy servers to avoid detections.

Proxy Chaining – Proxy chaining is a process which involves following the steps *(source – CEH Study Guide)*

a. User requests a resource from the destination or remote system.

b. Proxy Client at user's system connects to Proxy Server & passes the request to Proxy Server.

c. The Proxy Server strips the User's Identification information and passes request to next Proxy Server.

d. The process is repeated by all the Proxy Servers in the chain.

e. At the end unencrypted Request is passed to the web server and similar process happens while receiving back the information. The data travels through various chains to reach back to requesting user.

There are various proxy tools available such as –

1. Proxy Switcher
2. Proxy Workbench
3. **TOR – The Onion Router**
4. Cyber Ghost
5. VPN Gate
6. Open VPN
7. Nord VPN
8. Tunnel Bear
9. Hotspot Shield
10. Anonymizer
11. Socks Chain
12. Fiddler
13. Tails
14. G-Zapper, etc.

TOR – The Onion Browser

TOR was initially a project for a world wide network of services developed by the US Navy that enabled people to browse the internet anonymously. Now, It is a non-profit organization which aims for research and development of online privacy tools.

The TOR Network disguises your identity by moving your traffic across different TOR Servers and encrypting traffic, so it is not tracked back to you. Anyone who tries would see traffic coming from random nodes on the TOR network, rather than your actual computer system.

To access this network, you just need to download the TOR Browser, which is free to download from its official website. Everything you do in the browser goes through the TOR Network and doesn't need any setup or configuration from your side. Since your data goes through lots of relays, it's slow, and you will experience a much more sluggish internet than your usual connection.

It protects your identity by bouncing your communication around a distributed network of relays run by volunteers all around the world. It prevents somebody watching your connection from learning what sites you visit. It prevents sites you visit from learning your physical location, and it lets you access sites which are blocked and also *the deep & dark net.*

Tor can be used on Windows, MacOS, GNU/Linux without needing to install any other software except TOR Browser. It can also run off a USB flash drive which comes with a pre-configured web browser to protect your anonymity and is portable.

Summary

In this chapter, we have looked at various scanning methodology and used tools like Nmap & hping3. There is much practice required to master the art of scanning, especially optimal scanning. These scanning techniques are really helpful while performing Vulnerability Assessment & Penetration Testing (VAPT). We have learned various service scans such as TCP SYN Scan, TCP Connect Scan, Customized TCP Scan and performed Banner Grabbing using various tools.

In next chapter, we will look at basic terminologies and required know-how about vulnerability assessment.

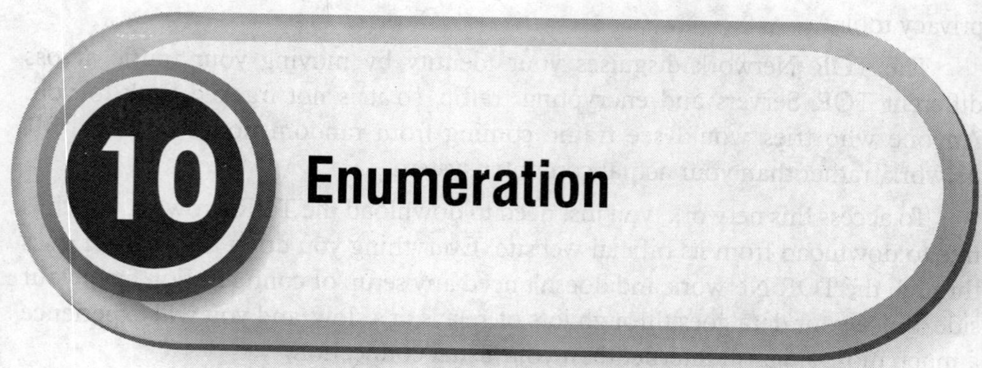

10 Enumeration

Enumeration is defined as systematic probing of the target with the intent of gathering information such as user environment and configuration. The enumeration helps the attacker to build a map of target machine so that it can be exploited. In this phase, the hacker tries to communicate with victim by connecting to services and gathering details about user details such as users, groups, routing table, password policy, banners, services, process, machine name, DNS etc.

The enumeration is performed on intranet network and identifies attacks points or loopholes in the target machine. It helps the hacker to connect to remote service and gain insights into the system as a user. The following are common services enumerated by hackers:

- Users
- Groups
- Password Policy
- Netbios Enumeration
- SNMP Enumeration
- Routing Tables
- Banners
- Services & Process
- SMTP & NTP Enumeration
- Network Shares
- DNS Enumeration
- Windows/Linux Enumeration

In the networking chapter, we had already discussed common Ports and services, now it's time to use them and gather detailed information about the target machine.

NetBIOS Enumeration (Windows)

NetBIOS is a commonly used service in Windows legacy systems used for gathering information about system services and common application/programs running the target machine. The NetBIOS API is used to for accessing and giving information about the resources that are been shared on the LAN. We are going to exploit this vulnerability in NetBIOS as it can result in serious loss of information such as disclosure of usernames, groups, password policy, services and domain info. It consists of 16-characters names where 15 characters identify machine name and last character identifies service on the machine. To enumerate NetBIOS we the default that should be 139 as it can information about the resources that is been shared and files shares which can lead to unauthorized access.

Windows Enumeration

The NetBIOS names are stored by Windows Internet Naming Service (WINS) which have ability to store and retrieve NETBIOS-IP mapping within the windows systems. There is command-line utility use for gathering NETBIOS information called nbtstat. The nbtstat is used for gathering information such as NETBIOS names, domain info, groups, services, protocols, session and users with the windows systems.

It is used for network maintenance and troubleshooting. Nbtstat is specially designed for name resolutions with associated IP Address.

Windows NetBIOS Enumeration using nbstat

a. Open command prompt & use following command to start nbtstat & check for various available options

```
Syntax-nbtstat/?
C:\Users\devansh>nbtstat/?
Displays protocol statistics and current TCP/IP
connections using NBT
(NetBIOS over TCP/IP).
NBTSTAT [ [-a Remote Name] [-A IP address] [-c]
[-n]
        [-r] [-R] [-RR] [-s] [-S] [interval]]
  -a (adapter status)-Lists the remote machine's
name table given its name
  -A (Adapter status)-Lists the remote machine's
name table given its IP address.
  -c (cache)-Lists NBT's cache of remote [machine]
names and their IP addresses
. . .
. . .
  Remote Name-Remote host machine name.
  IP address-Dotted decimal representation of the
IP address.
  Interval-Redisplays selected statistics, pausing
```

```
interval second between each display. Press Ctrl+C
to stop redisplaying statistics.
<end of command>
```

b. **C:\Users\devansh>nbstat -A 10.2.64.66**: To display the NetBIOS name table of a remote computer with the NetBIOS name.

NetBIOS connection states

- Connected: A session has been established.
- Associated: A connection endpoint has been created and associated with an IP address.
- Listening: This endpoint is available for an inbound connection.
- Idle: This endpoint has been opened but cannot receive connections.
- Connecting: A session is in the connecting phase and the name-to-IP address mapping of the destination is being resolved.
- Accepting: An inbound session is currently being accepted and will be connected shortly.
- Reconnecting: A session is trying to reconnect (it failed to connect on the first attempt).
- Outbound: A session is in the connecting phase and the TCP connection is currently being created.
- Inbound: An inbound session is in the connecting phase.
- Disconnecting: A session is in the process of disconnecting.
- Disconnected: The local computer has issued a disconnect and it is waiting for confirmation from the remote system.

NETBIOS Enumeration Using Linux

In Linux, there is command utility use for gathering NETBIOS information and also provides enumerate files shares and services on the system. The enum4linux is command-line tool used to enumerate users, password policy, shares. Enum4linux is a tool for enumerating information from Windows and Samba systems. It attempts to offer similar functionality to enum.exe formerly available from www.bindview.com.

a. Open command prompt & use the following command to start enum4linux also check for various available options –

```
Syntax- enum4linux
root@kali:~# enum4linux -h
enum4linux v0.8.9 (http://labs.portcullis.co.uk/
application/enum4linux/)
Copyright (C) 2011 Mark Lowe (mrl@portcullis-
security.com)
```

```
Simple wrapper around the tools in the samba
package to provide similar
functionality to enum.exe (formerly from www.
bindview.com). Some additional
features such as RID cycling have also been added
for convenience.
Usage: ./enum4linux.pl [options] ip
Options are (like "enum"):
    -U         get user list
    -M         get machine list*
    -S         get share list
    -P         get password policy information
    -G         get group and member list
    -d         be detailed, applies to -U and -S
    -u user    specify username to use (default "")
    -p pass    specify password to use (default "")
The following options from enum.exe aren't
implemented: -L, -N, -D, -f
Additional options:
    -a         Do all simple enumeration (-U -S -G
-P -r -o-i).
               This option is enabled if you don't
provide any other options.
    -h         Display this help message and exit
    -r         enumerate users via RID cycling
    -R range   RID ranges to enumerate (default:
500-550,1000-1050, implies -r)
    -K n       Keep searching RIDs until n
consecutive RIDs don't correspond to
               a username. Implies RID range ends
at 999999.
. . .
. . .
. . .
or "Network access: Allow anonymous SID/Name
translation" enabled (XP, 2003).
NB: Samba servers often seem to have RIDs in the
range 3000-3050.
Dependancy info: You will need to have the samba
package installed as this
script is basically just a wrapper around
rpcclient, net, nmblookup and smbclient. Polenum
from http://labs.portcullis.co.uk/application/
polenum/ is required to get Password Policy info.
```

```
<end of command>
```

b. **enum4linux -a 192.168.43.1** : -a switch retrieves all usernames, shares, password policy, domain, nbtstat info, groups.

Key Points

- The Tools used for Linux for gathering NETBIOS INFO are:

```
Enum4linux, Smbclient, Enum.
```

- The Tools used for Windows machine are nbtstat, netview, nbtscan, Superscan

NULL SESSIONS

The null sessions are special feature provided in windows machine which is used by the hackers to exploit the target machine by the connecting to an administrative share IPC$. The IPC$ share is an admin to share which has serve vulnerability as it allows the remote machine to connect to the share and comprise the authentication vulnerability in the windows system. The access to IPC share can create loss of information, leakage of data and even lead comprise of the system. The null session can lead remote procedure call and executing, running malicious API on the target machine. It can be used to facilitate the connection between systems on a network to allow one system to enumerate process and share on the victim. The null session creates special account null user that can reveal information about system shares and user accounts while not require a username and password for authentication purpose.

In Windows, we can connect to IPC$ share or create a null session by command-line utility called net use followed by UNC Path also providing a username, password.

- To connect to IPC share we use following command

```
C:\Users\devansh>Net use \\dev\ipc$ "" "/user:".
```

- To view the shares available on the particular system, after giving the following command to connect to IPC share on the target machine:

```
C:\Users\devan> net view \\dev.
```

- To connect to share on target machine:

```
C:\Users\devan> net use s: \\dev\ (shared folder
name)
```

PSTools Suite

The PSTools Suite is a command-line utility which provides the penetration tester to extract information and also perform system related task. The tools allow you to manage local and remote systems.

Download Link

https://technet.microsoft.com/en-us/sysinternals/bb896649.aspx

The tools contain various utilities or modules for extracting information about the machines.

- psExec - Executes process remotely
- psFile - Displays files opened remotely
- psInfo - Lists information about the system
- pskill - Kills process by name or process ID
- pslist - List detailed information about process
- psloggedon - Lets you see who's is logged into the system.
- psloglist - Dumps event log records
- pspasswd - Changes account password
- psservice - Views and control services
- psshutdown - Shutdown down and optionally reboots a computer

Linux Enumeration

Linux is free open source operating system developed by Linus Torvald using by Linux kernel and GNU utilities. The Linux has different distro or known as a distribution which a different variant of Linux, the only core difference is GNU utilities or Package Management Software. In Linux enumeration, we are going to focus our attention towards some basic Linux utilities and configuration we need to know in order to enumerate a Unix/Linux Machine.

Every time a user is created on Linux Machine, there are default settings which been auto-configured on the machine. The account has some values such as:

- Username & User ID (UID)
- Password
- Primary Group ID (GID) & name
- Secondary Group Name and GID
- Location of Home Directory
- Preferred shell
- The Linux password is stored in hash format MD5 or SHA within /etc/shadow which is only accessible to root user and contents cannot be modified by the user with fewer rights.
- The Linux user account information is stored in /etc/passwd file in a fixed format where different values are separated by the (:) and each entry for the user is recorded.
- Username: Password: UID: GID: Name: Home directory: Shell

- The root user has UID 0 and GID 0 and system accounts are also in a range of 100.
- The user can view their groups in /etc/group file and their hostname / etc/hostname.

Finger

The finger is a command-line utility which provides information about the users within the system, or it displays the logged-in user on the remote machine. The finger returns user home directory, login time, last time when they read the email, idle time etc.

The command parameters are <switches> and argument is username. The different switches are:

```
-b: removes home directory and shell
-f: removes header information from display
-l: returns the list of users.
-w: removes full name form display.
$ finger

Displays information about a user on a specified
system running the
Finger service. Output varies based on the remote
system.

FINGER [-l] [user]@host [...]

  -l        Displays information in long list
format.
  user      Specifies the user you want
information about. Omit the user
            parameter to display information about
all users on the
            specified host.
  @host     Specifies the server on the remote
system whose users you
            want information about.
```

RPCInfo

The rpcinfo helps the attacker to know what kind of information is leaked or disclosed on the remote system by Remote Procedure Call protocol. The RPC is a client-server architecture protocol used by the different programs to communicate and execute the process or performs computation. The p1 program requests or wants to execute a command on the remote system than it is sent to the local kernel via client stub and then interpreted by the remote machine stub and process get executed until that period the process in the client side is blocked or is waiting for response of the remote machine. This can lead to unwanted task or process getting executed on the target causing the system to leak information.

The command line for RPC looks as follows:

```
rpcinfo <switches> hostname
```

Switches that can be used are `-m` and `-s` for displaying the statistics for RPC on a given host and registered application and process that can be executed on the given host.

Showmounts

The showmount command list and identifies the shared directory present on a given system also it displays the clients having remotely mounted a file system.

The command line used for this showmount is given below:

```
showmount [-ade] [hostname]
-d: list directories that have been remotely
mounted by clients.
-e: prints list of shared directories.
-a: prints all the remote mounts done on the
system.
```

Simple Network Management Protocol (SNMP)

SNMP is defined as Simple Network Management Protocol, which was developed by the Internet Architecture Board (IAB) used for managing network devices such as switches, routers remotely. SNMP is a standard protocol used to manage and monitor network elements. The SNMP protocol uses default Port 161, 162 where 161 used for listening and 162 is used for receiving traps. There are 3 major versions of SNMP Protocol.

- SNMPv1- The version was used for managing network devices and while it lacked security aspect. There was no authentication and encryption involved during transmission of SNMP traps and messages.
- SNMPv2- This version included more functionality and management features but still less secure.
- SNMPv3: This version is the most secure and backward compatible. There are 2 key features in this version, authentication and encryption for ensuring secure communication.

Components of SNMP

- SNMP Agent
- SNMP Manager
- Management Information Base
- Manged Devices

SNMP Manager

SNMP manager software is a program that is used to manage communications with SNMP Agent and used to generate request/response in the form of traps. The SNMP Manager runs more than NMS software on given computer. The following are key features of SNMP Manager:

- Sending SNMP Traps
- Query SNMP Agent
- Set variable values for accessing and writing values to MIB.
- Acknowledges for asynchronous events from agents

Managed Devices

A managed device or the network element is a part of the network that requires some form of monitoring and management *e.g.* routers, switches, servers, workstations.

SNMP Agent

SNMP Agent is a program which includes managed device and network element as a whole and is used for querying MIB for reading and writing changes to Network Objects present in the computer network. Enabling the agent allows it to collect the management information database from the device locally and makes it available to the SNMP manager.

SNMP agent's key functions

- Collects management information about its local environment
- Stores and retrieves management information as defined in the MIB.
- Signals an event to the manager.
- Acts as a proxy for some non–SNMP manageable network node.

Management Information Base (MIB)

MIB is a database which contains hierarchically information about network objects or elements which can be managed by SNMP Manager. The MIB represents a standard representation of SNMP Agent information and configuration settings. The MIB elements are called Network Object Identifier is the numeric name given to object and begin with the root of tree. It is used to uniquely identify the network element. It contains MIB managed objects, including scalar objects that define singular and tabular objects to recognise groups of objects. The MIB includes object type, string, address, access level such as read/write size restrictions and range information. There are 2 passwords for SNMP both used to configure and read information form SNMP Agents. Read community string are used for reading values or configuration settings within MIB via password and these strings are public. The read/write community strings are used to changing configuration values and setting associated with network device. These are private community strings.

SNMP Commands

- GET: The GET operation is a request sent by the manager to the managed device. It is performed to retrieve one or more values from the managed device.
- SET: This operation is used by the managers to modify or assign the value of the Managed device.
- TRAPS: Unlike the above commands which are initiated from the SNMP Manager, TRAPS are initiated by the Agents. It is a signal to the SNMP Manager by the Agent on the occurrence of an event.
- INFORM: This command is similar to the TRAP initiated by the Agent, additionally INFORM includes confirmation from the SNMP manager on receiving the message.
- RESPONSE: It is the command used to carry back the value(s) or signal of actions directed by the SNMP Manager.

SNMP Enumeration

SNMP-check allows you to enumerate the SNMP devices and places the output in a very human readable friendly format. It could be useful for penetration testing or systems monitoring.

a. Open bash from the terminal and type the following command into shell snmp check -h for various help options.

```
root@kali:~# snmp-check -h
snmp-check v1.9 - SNMP enumerator
Copyright(c)2005-2015 by Matteo Cantoni (www.
nothink.org)
Usage: snmp-check [OPTIONS] <target IP address>
 -p --port: SNMP port. Default port is 161;
 -c --community: SNMP community. Default is
public;
 -v --version: SNMP version (1,2c). Default is 1;
 -w --write: detect write access (separate action
by enumeration);
 -d --disable_tcp: disable TCP connections
enumeration!
 -t --timeout: timeout in seconds. Default is 5;
 -r --retries: request retries. Default is 1;
 -i --info: show script version;
 -h --help: show help menu;
<end of command>
```

b. Scan the target host (192.168.1.2) using the public SNMP community string (-c public):

```
root@kali:~# snmp-check 192.168.1.2 -c public
snmp-check v1.9 - SNMP enumerator
Copyright (c) 2005-2015 by Matteo Cantoni (www.
nothink.org)
[+] Try to connect to 192.168.1.2:161 using SNMPv1
and community 'public'
[*] System information:
Host IP address                    : 192.168.1.2
  Hostname                         : ...retracted...
  Description                      : ...retracted...
  Contact                          : ...retracted...
  Location                         : ...retracted...
  Uptime snmp                      : -
  Uptime system                    : 3 days,
00:13:51.05
  System date                      : -
[*] Network information:
....SNIP...
[*] Network interfaces:
                                           ...
...
...
[*] TCP connections and listening ports:
....SNIP...
[*] Listening UDP ports:
....SNIP...
<end of command>
```

SNScan

SNScan is a utility which is used for detecting devices that have SNMP Agent on the network. The main function of the utility detects the devices and identify the vulnerability to carry out the SNMP Attacks. It checks for Ports 161,162 and also searches for the public, private strings, user-defined community strings.

DNS Enumeration

A zone transfer is a process where Authoritative Servers sends a copy of database file to another DNS Server. This method is used because it keeps the other DNS Servers updated about the DNS Quires received by them and sends back to resolver for caching purpose. In a DNS zone there is 1 Primary Server and others are Secondary Servers. The secondary server will ask the copy of zone file from the primary server so that information is updated.

The zone files consist of name-IP mapping where the hacker would know about the clients which are present on the internet which could lead to various attacks on the DNS Servers such DNS Poisoning where the DNS Entry values are manipulated to mislead the user to load the untrusted website. The attacker would know about the MX, NS, A, SOA, CNAME records which could leak DNS Servers information, Mail Servers, Directory Services, Network Devices, Domain-Controllers etc.

Windows DNS Enumeration

1. At Windows command line enter the following command nslookup and press enter.

```
C:\Users\devansh>nslookup
Default Server:  LAPTOP-F2NIEULD.mshome.net
Address:  192.168.137.1
```

2. The command prompt will change to > symbol and write set type= <record name>.

```
> set type=ns
```

3. The prompt now requires the following domain of the website for which are requesting the name server for e.g. www.google.com.

```
>> www.google.com
Server:  LAPTOP-F2NIEULD.mshome.net
Address:  192.168.137.1
google.com
primary name server = ns1.google.com
responsible mail addr = dns-admin.google.com
serial = 242354753
refresh = 900 (15 mins)
retry = 900 (15 mins)
expire = 1800 (30 mins)
default TTL = 60 (1 min)
<end of command>
```

4. Now enter ls- d <domain name> for DNS zone transfer, if the server is allowed to display or give copy of zone its show all the list of records and mapping associated with it.

Linux DNS Enumeration

1. At the command prompt enter dig <domain.com> axfr

   The transfer will either return all the records or message stating that following transfer is failed.
2. If command is successful the following output is displayed.

```
; <<>> DiG 9.13.3 <<>> linux.org
;; global options: +cmd
;; Got answer:
;; ->>HEADER<<- opcode: QUERY, status: NOERROR, id: 37159
;; flags: qr rd ra; QUERY: 1, ANSWER: 2, AUTHORITY: 2, ADDITIONAL: 5

;; OPT PSEUDOSECTION:
; EDNS: version: 0, flags:; udp: 4096
;; QUESTION SECTION:
;linux.org.                     IN      A

;; ANSWER SECTION:
linux.org.              300     IN      A       104.18.59.123
linux.org.              300     IN      A       104.18.58.123

;; AUTHORITY SECTION:
linux.org.              86379   IN      NS      lia.ns.cloudflare.com.
linux.org.              86379   IN      NS      mark.ns.cloudflare.com.

;; ADDITIONAL SECTION:
lia.ns.cloudflare.com.  84354   IN      A       173.245.58.185
lia.ns.cloudflare.com.  170762  IN      AAAA    2400:cb00:2049:1::adf5:3ab9
mark.ns.cloudflare.com. 170734  IN      A       173.245.59.130
mark.ns.cloudflare.com. 170734  IN      AAAA    2400:cb00:2049:1::adf5:3b82

;; Query time: 58 msec
;; SERVER: 192.168.1.1#53(192.168.1.1)
;; WHEN: Fri Oct 12 11:46:46 CEST 2018
;; MSG SIZE  rcvd: 212
```

Source-*https://linuxize.com/post/how-to-use-dig-command-to-query-dns-in-linux*

NTP Enumeration

NTP is defined as Network Time Protocol used for synchronizing time on the network between NTP Servers and networking devices. The important feature of NTP is to manage time while using directory services in order to log-on the systems. NTP utilizes UDP port 123. Through NTP enumeration we can gather information such as lists of hosts connected to NTP server, IP addresses, system names, and OS running on the client system in a LAN. All this information can be enumerated by querying NTP server. NTP works with UTC (Coordinated Universal Time) only and leaves the time zones up to endpoints to calculate. The following queries are used to query the NTP Servers:

- Ntpq
- Ntptrace
- Ntpdate
- Ntpdc

Nmap NSE Script

a. Open Command-Line and now we are going to perform UDP Scan on port 123. The following is a demonstrative output from nmap 'ntp-info' script against an NTP server:

```
root@devansh3008:~/$ sudo nmap -sU -p123 -iL ntp_
targ.txt --script ntp-info -Pn -n
Starting Nmap 6.25(http://nmap.org ) at 2013-08-27
18:01 NZST
Nmap scan report for 221.208.3.208
Host is up (0.70s latency).
PORT STATE SERVICE
123/udp open ntp
| ntp-info:
|_ receive time stamp: Tue Aug 27 18:01:21 2013
Nmap scan report for 46.181.154.179
Host is up (0.39s latency).
PORT STATE SERVICE
123/udp open ntp
| ntp-info:
| receive time stamp: Tue Aug 27 18:04:48 2013
| version: ntpd 4.2.4p0@1.1472 Thu Sep 9 05:32:12
UTC 2010 (1)
| processor: mips
| system: Linux/2.6.29.6-22-sigma
| leap: 0
| stratum: 3
| precision: -20
| rootdelay: 203.853
| rootdispersion: 79.939
| peer: 57326
| refid: 212.75.210.83
| reftime: 0xd5c6bda0.0af854e1
| poll: 10
| clock: 0xd5c6bff7.25966c4c
| state: 4
| offset: 0.369
| frequency: 32.927
| jitter: 0.145
| noise: 0.449
|_ stability: 0.015
<end of command>
```

NTPQ

The ntpq tool is a command-line application built to query and analyze remote ntpd daemons. ntpq can be run in both interactive (command-shell) mode, as well as directly issuing commands on the command-line via the -c parameter.

a. Open Command Line and enter the following command into the terminal ntpq with IP Address.

```
1)root@devansh3008 ntpq 99.112.40.155
current host is 99.112.40.155
2)ntpq> readlist
associd=0 status=06f4 leap_none, sync_ntp, 15
events, freq_mode,
version="ntpd 4.2.4p6@1.1549 Tue Jan 5 17:30:09
UTC 2010 (1)",
processor="mips", system="Linux/2.6.36.3",
leap=00, stratum=3,
precision=-14, rootdelay=41.225,
rootdispersion=83.750,
peer=32441,refid=68.94.156.17,reftime=d5c6be22.
fc081ca3 Tue, Aug 27 2013 17:56:50.984,
poll=10,clock=d5c6c35f.49747a0e Tue, Aug 27
2013 18:19:11.286, state=4,offset=0.359,
frequency=-31.472, jitter=0.897,
noise=4.232,stability=0.276
3)ntpq> lpeers
 remote refid st t when poll reach delay offset
jitter
===================================================
============
. . .
. . .
. . .
 1 32441 9634 yes yes none sys.peer reachable 3
 2 32442 9434 yes yes none candidate reachable 3
<end of command>
```

SMTP Enumeration

SMTP is known Simple Mail Transfer Protocol is used for sending mail and relies on Domain Service for transferring mail to from source to destination. It is an application layer protocol used in TCP/IP Stack. The SMTP Protocol uses default Port 25. SMTP is generally integrated within an email client application and 4 key components are:

1. A local user or client-end utility known as the mail user agent (MUA)
2. Server is known as mail submission agent (MSA)
3. Mail transfer agent (MTA)
4. Mail delivery agent (MDA)

SMTP Working

- The SMTP Server starts listening on port 25 for receiving mail from different hosts.

- The clients that want to send mail must establish a TCP connection with the mail server and inform the server that it would send a mail.
- The client sends a mail to destination IP Address or an MX Server where DNS lookups for the address of the following Mail Server and passes the request to mail server.
- The finally the message received with help of POP or IMAP Protocol and read by the receiver.

SMTP Features

- SMTP is a stateless Protocol.
- It uses connection-oriented protocol for establishing a connection to MX Server.
- The SMTP can handle only 7-bit ASCII Text and is also push protocol which means it can be used to send emails.
- Multipurpose Internet Email Extension (MIME) extends the functionality of SMTP by allowing users to send audio, video, graphics with an email attachment.
- SMTP cannot transfer executable files and binary objects.

Points to Note

SMTP enumeration allows us to determine valid users on the SMTP server. This is done with the help built-in SMTP commands, they are

- VRFY - This command is used for validating users.
- EXPN - This command tells the actual delivery address of aliases and mailing lists.
- RCPT TO - It defines the recipients of the message.

SMTP Enumeration Tools & Techniques

SMTP-Enum-User

Smtp-enum-user is command line utility used for enumerating user accounts on Unix/Linux systems. Enumeration is performed by inspecting the responses to VRFY, EXPN, and RCPT TO commands. Now we are going have look on the SMTP responses.

a. Open terminal and type the following command to view options.

```
root@devansh3008:~# smtp-user-enum -h
smtp-user-enum v1.2 ( http://pentestmonkey.net/
tools/smtp-user-enum )
Usage: smtp-user-enum.pl [options] ( -u username
| -U file-of-usernames ) ( -t host | -T file-of-
targets )
```

```
options are:
    -m n -Maximum number of processes (default: 5)
    -M -mode  Method to use for username guessing
EXPN, VRFY or RCPT (default: VRFY)
    -u -user  Check if user exists on remote
system
    -f addr - MAIL FROM email address.  Used only
in "RCPT TO" mode (default: user@example.com)
    -D dom - Domain to append to supplied user
list to make email addresses (Default: none)
     Use this option when you want to guess valid
email addresses instead of just usernames
     e.g. "-D example.com" would guess foo@
example.com, bar@example.com, etc.  Instead of
     simply the usernames foo and bar.
    -U file -File of usernames to check via smtp
service
    -t host -Server host running smtp service
. . .
. . .
-T file -File of hostnames running the smtp
service
<end of command>
```

b. Now we are going to search for specific user using -u and -M VERFY method to check user presence at particular mail server.

Now enter the following command using with IP Address of the target machine.

```
root@devansh3008:~# smtp-user-enum -M VRFY -u root
-t 192.168..43.23
Starting smtp-user-enum v1.2 ( http://
pentestmonkey.net/tools/smtp-user-enum )
 ----------------------------------------------------
|                 Scan Information
|
 ----------------------------------------------------
Mode ..................... VRFY
Worker Processes ......... 6
Target count ............ 1
Username count ........... 1
Target TCP port .......... 25
Query timeout ........... 4 secs
Target domain ...........
1 query in 1 seconds (1.0 queries / sec)
<end of command>
```

LDAP Enumeration

LDAP Stands for Lightweight Directory Access Protocol is used for accessing directory services, files or resources of the organization over the internet. The LDAP protocol uses TCP/IP implementation, and the default port for it is 389. The protocol is based on a client-server architecture and also uses X.500 directory services. LDAP including storing and retrieving data, searching for data matching a given set of criteria, authenticating clients. A directory server is a network database that is used to store information hierarchical. The information stored in LDAP is in the form of entity which has 3 values such as distinguished name, collection of attributes, collection of object classes.

Ad-Ldap-Enum

It is an Active Directory based enumeration tool used for locating users, groups and various directory services, files and resources on the network.

a. Open Kali machine and type the following command to see help options

```
Terminal - root@kali: ~/Desktop/ad-ldap-enum
File Edit View Terminal Tabs Help
root@kali:~/Desktop/ad-ldap-enum# python ad-ldap-enum.py -h
usage: ad-ldap-enum.py [-h] -l LDAP_SERVER -d DOMAIN [-a ALT_DOMAIN] [-e] [-n]
                       [-s] [-u USERNAME] [-p PASSWORD] [-v]
                       [-o FILENAME_PREPEND]

Active Directory LDAP Enumerator

optional arguments:
  -h, --help            show this help message and exit
  -v, --verbose         Display debugging information.
  -o FILENAME_PREPEND, --prepend FILENAME_PREPEND
                        Prepend a string to all output file names.

Server Parameters:
  -l LDAP_SERVER, --server LDAP_SERVER
                        IP address of the LDAP server.
  -d DOMAIN, --domain DOMAIN
                        Authentication account's FQDN. If an alternative
                        domain is not specified this will be also used as the
                        Base DN for searching LDAP.
  -a ALT_DOMAIN, --alt-domain ALT_DOMAIN
                        Alternative FQDN to use as the Base DN for searching
                        LDAP.
  -e, --nested          Expand nested groups.

Authentication Parameters:
```

Source- SecurityOnline

JX Explorer

JX Explorer is a free open source tool used for enumerating LDAP – enables directory. The JX Explorer helps to know about the directories and files listed within the Active Directory. The tool needs an JVM for installation and execution.

Other Tools

- LDAP Search

- NMAP
- LEX
- LDAP ADMIN TOOL

SSDP

SSDP protocol is defined as Simple Service Discovery Protocol is used for discovering of network services and Plug-N-Play devices (PNP). SSDP is a text-based protocol based on HTTPU and uses UDP as the underlying transport protocol. Network devices can find and communicate with each other by plugging them in or turning them on, allowing them to ''play'' with minimal configuration on the part of the owner. It allows the peripheral devices to communicate over LAN. The default Port for SSDP is 1900.

Active Directory (AD)

Active Directory is a Windows Microsoft product which is used to restrict resources on the network and also provides security based on different permissions. The AD stores data as an object. An object can be user, group, device etc. The object is identified by its name and attributes. The AD also Domain Services, which is used to store information as directory and is used to manage user interaction with the domain.

The Active Directory provides several features or services such as

- Domain Services
- LDAP Services
- CA Services
- Directory Federation Services
- Rights Management

Summary

This module covers the enumeration process and the information gained by the hacker to exploit the machine. The various enumeration techniques were used for Linux and Windows machine. The common ports and services such as SMTP, SNMP, LDAP, NTP, NETBIOS, DNS Enumeration were performed in order to reveal the user accounts, process, routing, mail records etc were collected for exploitation phase. The next chapter we will look at basic know-how about vulnerability assessment & penetration testing.

11 Introduction to Vulnerability Assessment

Module Outline

- Introduction to Vulnerability Assessment & Penetration Testing
- Six Step Process for Vulnerability Assessment
- Types & Scope of Vulnerability Assessment
- Burp Suite & it's Basics Usage
- Acunetix
- OWASP Zed Attack Proxy (ZAP)

Vulnerability Assessment is an important process which involves the discovery of potential threats and loopholes or vulnerability, which might lead to issues such as sensitive data leakage, security breach or even complete system takeover. It is carried out based on the intel discovered using various Information Gathering, Scanning & Enumeration Techniques. The first phase of any penetration testing process is to gather as much as possible intel about the overall architecture of target, which involves basic details to advance information such as open ports, services running, etc.

In Vulnerability Assessment, we look for vulnerable endpoints that might be present in the open ports or the service discovered during the scanning phase or it might be possible to hack into target just by social engineering a sensitive employee.

Since, the scope of this book is about mastering Information Gathering & Scanning Techniques, but it is extended to give you additional information about vulnerability assessment. There will be another edition of this book which will be specific to Vulnerability Assessment Process (consider as second part of the book or second volume).

In this chapter, we will look at basic know-how about vulnerability assessment, common terminologies and basic idea, how it is carried out, the scope of VAPT, types of VAPT and some basic automated testing tools for performing VAPT. By this chapter, you must have gained a solid understanding of working with different operating systems and working knowledge about using various tools and techniques.

Vulnerability Assessment & Penetration Testing

Vulnerability Assessment & Penetration Testing are two processes which often goes hand in hands. These two plays an important role from the security perspective of an organization as well as for ensuring overall security posture.

Vulnerability Assessment is a process which involves identifying loopholes/ vulnerable points in a target system which may give the attacker an advantage to exploit the target. It also tells how it might be exploited through the vulnerability found.

According to Comodo, Vulnerability Assessment as the name suggests is the process of recognizing, analysing and ranking vulnerabilities in computers and other related systems to equip the IT personnel and management team with adequate knowledge about prevailing threats in the environment. With the appropriate information at hand, the risk factors can rightly be understood, and the required measures can be defined competently without any delay. Vulnerability Assessment is not specific to one industry and can be applied in all industries ranging from IT systems to Energy and other utility systems.

According to Veracode, Vulnerability Assessment and Penetration Testing (VAPT) are two types of vulnerability testing. The tests have different strengths and are often combined to achieve a more complete vulnerability analysis. In short, Penetration Testing and Vulnerability Assessments perform two different tasks, usually with different results, within the same area of focus.

Vulnerability assessment tools discover which vulnerabilities are present, but they do not differentiate between flaws that can be exploited to cause damage and those that cannot. Vulnerability scanners alert companies to the pre-existing flaws in their code and where they are located. Penetration tests attempt to exploit the vulnerabilities in a system to determine whether unauthorized access or other malicious activity is possible and identify which flaws pose a threat to the application. Penetration tests find exploitable flaws and measure the severity of each. A penetration test is meant to show how damaging a flaw could be in a real attack rather than find every flaw in a system. Together, penetration testing and vulnerability assessment tools provide a detailed picture of the flaws that exist in an application and the risks associated with those flaws.

If vulnerabilities are found as a part of any assessment then there is a need for disclosure. Generally, such disclosures are carried out by separate teams like **Computer Emergency Readiness Team (CERT)** or the organizations which has discovered the vulnerability.

Six Step Vulnerability Assessment Process

1. Spot & realize the approach of your industry or system like how it is structured and managed.
2. Trace the systems, data and applications that are exercised throughout the practice of the business.

3. Investigate the unseen data sources which can permit simple entry to the protected information.
4. Classify both the physical and virtual servers that run the necessary business applications.
5. Tracking all the existing security measures which are already implemented.
6. Inspect the network for any vulnerability.

Types of Vulnerability Assessment

(Source – Comodo)

Basically, a vulnerability assessment applies various methods, tools, and scanners to find out grey areas, threats, and risks. Everything depends on how well the weakness in the given systems is discovered to attend to that specific need. Find below different types of vulnerability assessment scans.

1. Network Based Scans

Going by the name, it helps identify possible network security attacks. The scan helps zero-in the vulnerable systems on wired or wireless networks.

2. Host Based Scans

Server workstations or other network hosts vulnerabilities are easily identified using these scans. In the process, ports and services are examined vigorously. It also provides excellent visibility into the configuration settings and patch history of scanned systems.

3. Wireless Network Scans

Wireless network infrastructure is scanned to identify vulnerabilities, it helps in validating a company's network.

4. Application Scans

It is used to test websites to discover all known software vulnerabilities.

5. Database Scans

Database Scans aid in identifying grey areas in a database to prevent vicious attacks by cybercriminals.

Scope of Vulnerability Assessment

While appearing checks and tests, the scope of the task wishes to be simply defined. The scope is primarily based on the assets to be tested. The following are the 3 viable scopes that exist.

Black Box Testing: Testing from an external network with no prior expertise of the internal networks and systems.

Gray Box Testing: Checking out from an external or inner network, with knowledge of the internal networks and systems. This is usually an aggregate of black box testing and white box testing.

White Container Testing: Performing the test from within the network with the understanding of the community architecture and the structures. This is also called internal testing.

Popular Vulnerability Assessment Tools

1. Burp Suite

Burp Suite is an integrated platform for performing security testing of web applications. Its various tools work seamlessly together to support the entire testing process, from initial mapping and analysis of an application's attack surface, through to finding and exploiting security vulnerabilities. Burp gives you full control, letting you combine advanced manual techniques with state-of-the-art automation, to make your work faster, more effective, and more fun.

Burp suite free edition comes pre-installed with Kali Linux & can be downloaded for other operating systems as well. It will require Java dependencies to work.

The basics of using Burp Suite

(source - https://portswigger.net/burp/documentation/desktop/penetration-testing)

To use Burp for penetration testing, you need to configure your browser to work with Burp, and install Burp's CA certificate in your browser.

Once you have Burp running and configured your browser, go to the **Proxy Intercept tab**, and ensure that interception is **turned on** (if the button says "Intercept is off" then click it to toggle the interception status). Then go to your browser and visit any URL.

Each HTTP request made by your browser is displayed in the Intercept taYou can view each message, and edit it if required. You then click the "Forward" button to send the request on to the destination web server. If at any time there are intercepted messages pending, you will need to forward all of these in order for your browser to complete loading the pages it is waiting for. You can toggle the "Intercept is on / off" button in order to browse normally without any interception, if you require.

As you browse an application via Burp, the Proxy history keeps a record of all requests and responses. In the Proxy, go to the History tab and review the series of requests you have made. Select an item in the table and view the full messages in the Request and Response tabs.

Also, as you browse, Burp by default builds up a site map of the target application. Go to the Target tab, and the Site Map sub-tab, to view this. The site map contains all of the URLs you have visited in your browser, and also all of the content that Burp has inferred from responses to your requests (*e.g.* by parsing links from HTML responses). Items that have been requested are shown in black, and other items are shown in gray.

At the core of Burp's penetration testing workflow is the ability to pass HTTP requests between the Burp tools, to carry out particular tasks. You can send messages from the Proxy intercept tab, the Proxy history, the site map, and indeed anywhere else in Burp that you see HTTP messages. To do this, select one or more messages, and use the context menu to send the request to another tool.

The Burp tools you will use for particular tasks are as follows:

Scanner - This is used to automatically scan websites for content and security vulnerabilities.

Intruder - This allows you to perform customized automated attacks, to carry out all kinds of testing tasks.

Repeater - This is used to manually modify and reissue individual HTTP requests over and over.

Collaborator client - This is used to generate Burp Collaborator payloads and monitor for resulting out-of-band interactions.

Clickbandit - This is used to generate clickjacking exploits against vulnerable applications.

Sequencer - This is used to analyze the quality of randomness in an application's session tokens.

Decoder - This lets you transform bits of application data using common encoding and decoding schemes.

Comparer - This is used to perform a visual comparison of bits of application data to find interesting differences.

You can combine Burp's different tools in numerous ways, to perform testing tasks ranging from very simple to highly advanced and specialized.

Tool configuration - Burp contains a wealth of configuration options, which it is often necessary to use at different stages of your testing, to ensure that Burp works with your target application in the way you require. For example:

Display - You can configure the font and character set used to display HTTP messages, and also the font in Burp's own UI.

Target scope - The target scope configuration tells Burp the items that you are currently interested in and willing to attack. You should configure this early in your testing, as it can control which items are displayed in the Proxy history and Target site map, which messages are intercepted in the Proxy, and which items may be scanned.

Platform authentication - If the application server employs any platform level (HTTP) authentication, you configure Burp to handle the authentication automatically.

Session handling - Many applications contain features that can hinder automated or manual testing, such as reactive session termination, use of per-request tokens, and stateful multi-stage processes. You can configure Burp to handle most of these situations seamlessly, using a combination of session handling rules and macros.

Task scheduling - You can configure Burp to schedule tasks at given times or intervals, to allow you to work within specified testing windows.

2. *Acunetix Web Vulnerability Scanner*

Website: www.acunetix.com

Acunetix Web Vulnerability Scanner includes many innovative features:

1. AcuSensor Technology
2. An automatic client script analyser allowing for security testing of Ajax and Web 2.0 applications.
3. Industries' most advanced and in-depth SQL injection and Cross site scripting testing.
4. Advanced penetration testing tools, such as the HTTP Editor and the HTTP Fuzzer.
5. Visual macro recorder makes testing web forms and password protected areas easy
6. Support for pages with CAPTHCA, single sign-on and Two Factor authentication mechanisms.
7. Extensive reporting facilities including VISA PCI compliance reports.
8. Multi-threaded and lightning fast scanner crawls hundreds of thousands of pages with ease.
9. Intelligent crawler detects web server type and application language.
10. Acunetix crawls and analyses websites including flash content, SOAP and AJAX.
11. Port scans a web server and runs security checks against network services running on the server.

3. *OWASP Zed Attack Proxy (ZAP)*

The OWASP Zed Attack Proxy (ZAP) is one of the world's most popular free security tools and is actively maintained by hundreds of international volunteers*. It can help you automatically find security vulnerabilities in your web applications while you are developing and testing your applications. It is also a great tool for experienced pentesters to use for manual security testing.

Some of ZAP 's features:

- Intercepting Proxy
- Automated scanner
- Passive scanner
- Brute Force scanner

- Spider
- Fuzzer
- Port scanner
- Dynamic SSL certificates
- API
- Beanshell integration

For more information about ZAP

https://www.owasp.org/index.php/OWASP_Zed_Attack_Proxy_Project

4. Web Application Attack and Audit Framework (W3af)

W3af is an extremely popular, powerful, and flexible framework for finding and exploiting web application vulnerabilities. It is easy to use and extend and features dozens of web assessment and exploitation plugin

As a framework w3af provides developers that want to extend it via plugins the following features:

A. Daemons

Our framework implements web and proxy servers which are easy to integrate into your code in order to identify and exploit vulnerabilities.

B. Fast HTTP Client

w3af has wrapped urllib2 in a thread-safe way and with lots of extensions (Keep-Alive, Gzip, Logging, etc.) which allow you to send specially crafted HTTP requests at lightning speeds. Other features offered by the HTTP client are:

- Proxy support
- HTTP Basic and Digest authentication
- UserAgent faking
- Add custom headers to requests
- Cookie handling
- HTTP response cache
- DNS cache
- File upload using multipart

C. Output Manager

Logging is one of the most important features of any framework and we've developed various types of logging methods for you to consume in the custom code. Output can be written to:

- Console
- Text, CSV, HTML and XML files
- Sent by email

The XML file is ideal for you to integrate w3af into your company SDLC, since it provides all the information about the vulnerabilities that were detected during the scan Vulnerability name, Vulnerability description, HTTP requests and responses, etc. and validates against our XSD.

D. Fuzzing engine

w3af can inject your payloads into almost every part of the HTTP request:

- Query string
- POST-data
- Headers
- Cookie values
- Multipart/form file content
- URL filename
- URL path

The fuzzing engine can be configured using the misc-settings menu, since not all of these injection points are enabled by default, make sure you check which ones you need before starting a scan.

E. Knowledge base

All vulnerabilities, information disclosures, and anything valuable identified by one plugin will be stored in a knowledge base which is accessible by all the other plugins. Writing a plugin that requires a XSS vulnerability to run? No problem, simply add the audit.xss plugin as a dependency and wait for it to store the vulnerabilities into the KB.

F. Parsing

The framework tries very hard to parse and extract links and forms from any HTML that's found during the crawling phase. Support for various encodings and broken HTML tags is built-in.

Summary

In this chapter, we have explored about vulnerability assessment, it's types, scope & process of performing vulnerability assessment and penetration testing. Apart from this, we have also looked at primary usage of one of the essential tools *i.e.* Burp Suite & some other automated scanners such as Acunetix & open source tool OWASP Zed Attack Proxy.

Bonus Chapter: Additional References & Resources

1. **Awesome Social Engineering** – A curated list of awesome social engineering resources, inspired by the awesome–* trend on GitHuThose resources and tools are intended only for cybersecurity professional, penetration testers and educational use in a controlled environment.

   Resource Link – https://github.com/v2–dev/awesome–social–engineering

2. **Th3Inspector** – It is a tool used for Information Gathering & Reconnaissance.

   Resource Link –https://github.com/Moham3dRiahi/Th3inspector

3. **RedHawk** – All in one tool for Information Gathering, Vulnerability Scanning and Crawling. A must have tool for all penetration testers.

   Resource Link –https://github.com/Tuhinshubhra/RED_HAWK

4. **Raccoon** – Offensive Security Tool for Reconnaissance and Information Gathering

   Resource Link – https://github.com/evyatarmeged/Raccoon

5. **Trape** – People tracker on the Internet: OSINT analysis and research tool by Jose Pino.

   Resource Link – https://github.com/jofpin/trape

6. **ADRecon** – ADRecon is a tool which extracts and combines various artefacts (as highlighted below) out of an AD environment. The information can be presented in a specially formatted Microsoft Excel report that includes summary views with metrics to facilitate analysis and provide a holistic picture of the current state of the target AD environment.

   Resource Link – https://github.com/sense–of–security/ADRecon

7. **Penetration Testers Framework (PTF)** – The Penetration Testers Framework (PTF) is a way for modular support for up–to–date tools.

   Resource Link – https://github.com/trustedsec/ptf

8. **FSociety Hacking Tools Packs** – A Penetration Testing Framework, you will have every script that a hacker needs. Fsociety Contains All Tools Used in Mr. Robot Series.

   Resource Link – https://github.com/Manisso/fsociety

9. **Faraday** – Collaborative Penetration Test and Vulnerability Management Platform.
   Resource Link – https://github.com/infobyte/faraday
10. **Cyber Laws in India** – http://www.cyberlawsindia.net/
11. **Penetration Testing Report Template** – http://www.vulnerabilityassessment.co.uk/report%20template.html
12. **Siofra** – Siofra is a tool designed to identify and exploit DLL hijacking vulnerabilities in Windows programs. It is able to simulate the Windows loader in order to give visibility into all of the dependencies (and corresponding vulnerabilities) of a PE on disk, or alternatively an image file in memory corresponding to an active process.
   Resource Link – https://github.com/Cybereason/siofra
13. **Rootkits List** – This is the list of all rootkits found so far on GitHub and other sites.
   Resource Link – https://github.com/d30sa1/RootKits–List–Download
14. **Machine Learning for Cyber Security** – A curated list of amazingly awesome tools and resources related to the use of machine learning for cyber security.
   Resource Link – https://github.com/jivoi/awesome–ml–for–cybersecurity
15. **Bug Bounty Cheat Sheet** – https://github.com/EdOverflow/bugbounty–cheatsheet
16. **Awesome Bug Bounty** – A comprehensive curated list of Bug Bounty Programs and write–ups from the Bug Bounty hunters.
   Resource Link – https://github.com/djadmin/awesome–bug–bounty
17. **Security Tools by BL4DE** – Collection of small security tools created mostly in Python. CTFs, pentests and so on.
   Resource Link – https://github.com/bl4de/security–tools
18. **Awesome CTF** – A curated list of Capture the Flag (CTF) frameworks, libraries, resources, software and tutorials. This list aims to help starters as well as seasoned CTF players to find everything related to CTFs at one place.
   Resource Link – https://github.com/apsdehal/awesome–ctf
19. **Hacking Tools Repository by Gexos** – A list of security/hacking tools that have been collected from the internet.
   Resource Link – https://github.com/Gexos/Hacking–Tools–Repository
20. **HackDroid** – A Collection of Penetration Testing Apps for Android.
   Resources Link – https://github.com/thehackingsage/HackDroid
21. **H4cker GitHub Repository** – This repository is primarily maintained by Omar Santos and includes resources related to ethical hacking / penetration testing, digital forensics and incident response (DFIR), vulnerability research, exploit development, reverse engineering, and more

Resource Link – https://github.com/The–Art–of–Hacking/h4cker

Please Note – You can find list of all the links mentioned in this book at: www.cybersquareinfo.com/masteringaigs

Additional Textbook & Web Reference

1. https://www.hackingarticles.in/understanding-http-protocol/ [CH – 3, HTTP Status Code]
2. https://www.tutorialspoint.com/python/python_http_response.htm [CH – 3, HTTP Status Code]
3. http://mars.netanya.ac.il/~unesco/cdrom/booklet/HTML/NETWORKING/node300.html [CH - 3, The Telnet Protocol]
4. https://www.dedgepromotions.in/remote-desktop-protocol-rdp/ [CH – 3, RDP]
5. https://www.myce.com/news/kaspersky-hackers-try-to-take-over-pcs-running-remote-desktop-software-72132/ [CH – 3, RDP]
6. https://en.wikipedia.org/wiki/Remote_Desktop_Protocol [CH – 3, RDP]
7. https://www.webopedia.com/TERM/F/ftp.html [CH – 3, FTP]
8. http://docshare.tips/cehv8-module-04-enumeration_5749124fb6d87fb00d8b46e1.html [CH – 3, SMB]
9. https://vdocuments.mx/cehv8-module-04-enumerationpdf.html [CH – 3, NetBIOS]
10. https://whois.icann.org/en/primer [CH – 6, Whois Information]
11. https://archive.org/about/ [CH – 6, Archive.org]
12. https://mxtoolbox.com/domain [CH – 6, Domain Health Report]
13. https://mxtoolbox.com/SubnetCalculator.aspx [CH – 6, Subnet Calculator]
14. http://stalkscan.com/ [CH – 7, Stalkscan.com]
15. http://www.windowscommandline.com/nbstat-command-windows-command-line/ [CH – 10, Nbstat]
16. https://www.manageengine.com/network-monitoring/what-is-snmp.html [CH – 10, SNMP]
17. https://tools.kali.org/information-gathering/snmp-check [CH – 10, SNScan]
18. https://www.greycampus.com/opencampus/ethical-hacking/smtp-enumeration [CH – 10, SMTP Enumeration Tools & Techniques]
19. https://enterprise.comodo.com/blog/what-is-vulnerability-assessment/ [CH – 11, Vulnerability Assessment & Penetration Testing]
20. https://enterprise.comodo.com/blog/what-is-vulnerability-assessment/ [CH – 11, Vulnerability Assessment & Penetration Testing]
21. https://www.softwaretestinghelp.com/vulnerability-assessment-tools/ [CH – 11, Six Step Vulnerability Assessment Process]

END NOTE

Cyber Security is an essential component in the digital world. It is required to learn all the know–how about cyber security protection methodology, privacy protection, and securing your identity over the network. With growing data breaches and risks which are increasing exponentially, there is a requirement of the responsible and qualified security professional in good numbers.

Cyber security is an art as well as skill to master. Only single part of this might be dangerous for the target or the individual.

I highly recommend from my personal experiences to continually practice for a long run about various tactics, technologies and tools.

I wish all the readers best wishes to pursue their career into Cyber Security & Intelligence Domain and looking forward to seeing them turned into exceptional & knowledgeable professionals using best of their knowledge for the welfare of their country.

Thank you for spending your precious time and bucks on this book.

— Harsh Bothra